PERSONAL WORKBOOK
TO ACCOMPANY

THE PROFESSIONAL COUNSELOR

PERSONAL WORKBOOK
TO ACCOMPANY

Hackney and Cormier
THE PROFESSIONAL COUNSELOR
A PROCESS GUIDE TO HELPING
THIRD EDITION

JOHN L. GARCIA
SOUTHWEST TEXAS STATE UNIVERSITY

ALLYN AND BACON
BOSTON • LONDON • TORONTO • SYDNEY • TOKYO • SINGAPORE

Copyright © 1996, 1993 by Allyn & Bacon
A Simon & Schuster Company
Needham Heights, Massachusetts 02194

All rights reserved. No part of the material protected by this copyright may be reproduced or utilized in any form or by any means, electronic or mechanical, including photocopying, recording, or by any information storage and retrieval system, without the written permission of the copyright owner.

ISBN 0-205-19543-1

Printed in the United States of America

10 9 8 7 6 5 4 3 2 1   00 99 98 97 96 95

CONTENTS

Preface ii

To the user iii

PART ONE   Who Are You and What Is Calling You To Become a Counselor, and Why Now? 1

PART TWO   What Is Counseling? 47

PART THREE   Stages and Skills of Counseling 63

    Rapport and Relationship 91

    Assessing Client Problems 102

    Developing Counseling Goals 117

    Defining Strategies and Interventions 126

    Dancing with the Interventions 133

    Termination 140

    Applying Counseling Skills to Unique Situations 146

PART FOUR   The Foundation of It All - A Code of Ethics and Beyond 147

References 158

PREFACE

ABOUT THIS WORKBOOK

This is a most intimate book. It is all about YOU - the resources, unique qualities, and, of equal importance, the personal limitations you might bring to the noble art and ever-emerging technology of professional counseling. It is not designed to provide answers. Rather, it is intended to assist you in asking better questions about yourself and your relationship to your work. Thereby, it adheres to the underlying philosophy of the textbook which it accompanies - *counseling as process*. Use this workbook wisely. Keep it. And perhaps, years from now when its pages are torn and tattered, you will bring it out and respond afresh to the ideas it poses.

Counseling is an inter-personal activity. Therefore the person of the counselor emerges as the primary vehicle for the delivery of any counseling technique. The exercises found herein are designed to assist you as a beginning student of counseling not only in acquiring information about its technology, but also in discovering more about who you are as a person, and how you have arrived at the place to be trained as a professional helper. Maybe this workbook will help you better prepare yourself for the challenges you will face in a professional helping career.

You may notice that this book tends to repeat itself in places - and that is *by design*. Your road to maturity as a professional counselor will necessarily wind through the same location many times. Be patient with this reality.

The workbook is designed to be used with the third edition of *The Professional Counselor: A Process Guide to Helping* by Hackney & Cormier, and is arranged in four parts:

Who are You and What Is Calling You to Become A Counselor, and Why Now?

What is Counseling? (Chapter 1, Hackney & Cormier)

Stages and Skills of Counseling (Chapters 2 through 12, Hackney & Cormier)

The Foundation of It All - A Code of Ethics and Beyond

Students are encouraged to personalize the material in this workbook as much as possible - both *intra-* and *inter-*personally. For example, the exercises may first be completed in solitude allowing for personal reflection, and then perhaps brought into dialogue, when appropriate, with fellow students, your professor, and your therapist, for amplification and further application. No exercise in this workbook is intended to be complete in and of itself, but rather to open pathways for deeper understanding and acceptance of one's own process and its impact on the enterprise of professional helping.

TO THE USER

Some of the exercises contained in this workbook are of my own creation. Others are a synthesis of bits and pieces that I have acquired and found useful over the years in counselor education. Wherever possible I have given credit to the original source of the exercise or idea. I invite you to advise me of any sources I have overlooked.

Special thanks to Katherine McIver without whose assistance these pages would still be in my head. Kathie provided the book design and computer graphics, as well as research, word processing, and encouragement.

This book is dedicated to my students - *past, present, and future*.

John L. Garcia
San Marcos, Texas

Dig into yourself for a deep answer. And if this answer rings out in assent, if you meet this solemn question with a strong, simple, *"I must,"* then build your life in accordance with this necessity . . . .

. . . .

. . . . But after this descent into yourself and into your solitude, perhaps you will have to renounce becoming a poet [counselor] (if, as I have said, one feels one could live without writing [helping], then one shouldn't write [help] at all). Nevertheless, even then, this self-searching will not have been for nothing. Your life will still find its own paths from there, and that they may be good, rich, and wide is what I wish for you, more than I can say.

Rainer Maria Rilke
Paris, 1903.
From: *Letters to A Young Poet*

PERSONAL WORKBOOK
TO ACCOMPANY

THE PROFESSIONAL COUNSELOR

PART ONE

WHO ARE YOU AND WHAT IS CALLING YOU TO BECOME A COUNSELOR; AND *WHY NOW*?

"Self-knowledge includes full awareness of relationship to the ancestors, the yet unborn, nature, and community "(Myers, et al. 1991, p. 58)

Before it can be possible to know where you might be going as a professional helper, it is necessary to know where you have come from and what you bring to the training. Take some time for yourself and work through the following exercises.

1. **Write your full birth name here:**

    _____

   A. What is the significance of this name? Were you named for someone else? Who? What was that person like? What occupation did that individual assume? Do you like your name?

   B. Do you have any nicknames? If so, what is their significance? Who assigned the name(s) to you?

   C. Where were you born? Into what kind of culture? What was the *Zeitgeist* of the country at the time you were born?

   D. Where are you in the life-cycle? What about this could be influencing your decision to seek training as a professional helper now?

   _____
   _____
   _____
   _____
   _____
   _____
   _____
   _____
   _____
   _____

2 Personal Workbook

2. **Write your autobiography.** Sit down at your computer, or with pen and paper, and begin writing the story of your life. Start with conception. Where were you conceived? What was the context of your conception (i.e., the nature of the relationship between your birth parents)? What was your birth like (i.e., was it medically assisted; in a hospital, at home, or somewhere else)? Were you breast- or bottle-fed? What was your toilet training like? You may want to interview persons who took care of you during the early developmental years. What was starting to school like? If you can find teachers who knew you then, talk with them and ask what kind of a child you were. Go through middle childhood, adolescence, early adulthood, and on to wherever you are now. What have your relationships been like? What kinds of gains and losses have you sustained along the way? Try not to censor the story; simply free associate. Once you have finished, consider what you would edit if someone else were going to read what you have written (e.g., your professor). What would direct you to make these changes? What kinds of feelings do you notice as you make deletions and additions?

3. **Create your family genogram.** A genogram is a tri-generational schematic of the family tree. See McGoldrick, M. & Gerson, R. (1985). *Genograms in family assessment*. New York: Norton, for more information.

    Use a large piece of newsprint paper, crayons, markers, etc., and be more concerned about comprehensive information than neatness. Once the genogram is completed, place it on a wall, on your refrigerator, or anywhere you can see it daily as you go through your professional training. Look for patterns of relationship, incidence of particular physical manifestations (e.g., hypertension, alcoholism, epilepsy, etc.,), and roles traditionally assumed by males and females that could impact your work as a professional helper.

4. **What do you look like?** Place a recent photograph of yourself below.

    Mainstream United States is a material-focused society and thus tends to place emphasis on visual images. What might your image communicate to those who come to you for counseling? Look closely at your photograph. Based solely on appearance, *would you go to this person for help?*

Write a letter to your physical body. Start with *"Dear Body...."* You may begin with your feet, move up your legs, to your thighs, genitals, buttocks, stomach, arms, breasts, shoulders, neck, face, complexion, lips, eyes, nose, mouth, teeth, eyebrows, forehead, and hair. Tell each part what you like and dislike about it. What would you change if you could?

Personal Workbook

5. **Top-Ten List.** Tear off ten relatively large strips of paper. On these strips write the *ten most important factors in your life* - one per strip of paper. The factors may be people (do not use broad terms like "children" or "family" - be specific; use names and only one per strip), material items such as money, career, or maybe ideals such as integrity. Just consider what is important to you and write each one on a piece of paper. Once you have all ten done, look through them - let the mind's eye pass over them. How did these come to be so important to you?

Now, place a wastebasket near you and pretend that, through no fault of your own - just because life is not always fair - ONE of these factors had to be taken away forever. What would go first? Once you have decided, wad the paper up and toss it into the wastebasket. Look at what is left. How would your life now be different? Now, from the remaining nine, do the same thing again. With these eight, how would your life be different? Do the same thing again, all the way to the *one most important aspect of your life.* Consider the resources you would call upon to *adjust/adapt* to each new situation (D'Andrea, 1983).

Pay attention to your emotions as you go through this exercise. Notice the nature of the resistance you experience as you eliminate each aspect all the way to the final choice. Once you have reached the single most important aspect of your life, write what or who it is on the line below.

How might this factor impact and be impacted by your work as a professional counselor?

_____
_____
_____
_____
_____
_____
_____
_____
_____
_____

6. **Childhood Fantasies.** When you were little, what did you dream about becoming when you grew up (e.g., nurse, doctor, homemaker, firefighter, soldier)? How does your decision now to pursue a career in professional counseling relate to those early dreams?

Personal Workbook

7. **Paradise Lost.** As you look at your life now, what early dreams are (due to age, family responsibilities, physical limitations, financial resources, etc.) no longer available to you? How have you grieved these lost dreams? How does a career in the counseling profession perhaps relate to these losses?

Part 1   Who? What? and Why Now?   **7**

8. **My Essential Self.** Much has been written about the *self*, and we hear this term tossed around popularly now. What does it really mean? Based on the work of Heinz Kohut (1971; 1977) and adapted here from Baker & Baker (1987), the "tri-polar self" represents "the center of the individual's psychological universe" (Kohut, 1977, p. 311). The three aspects of self are one's *talents*, one's *ambitions*, and one's *goals*. Complete the following:

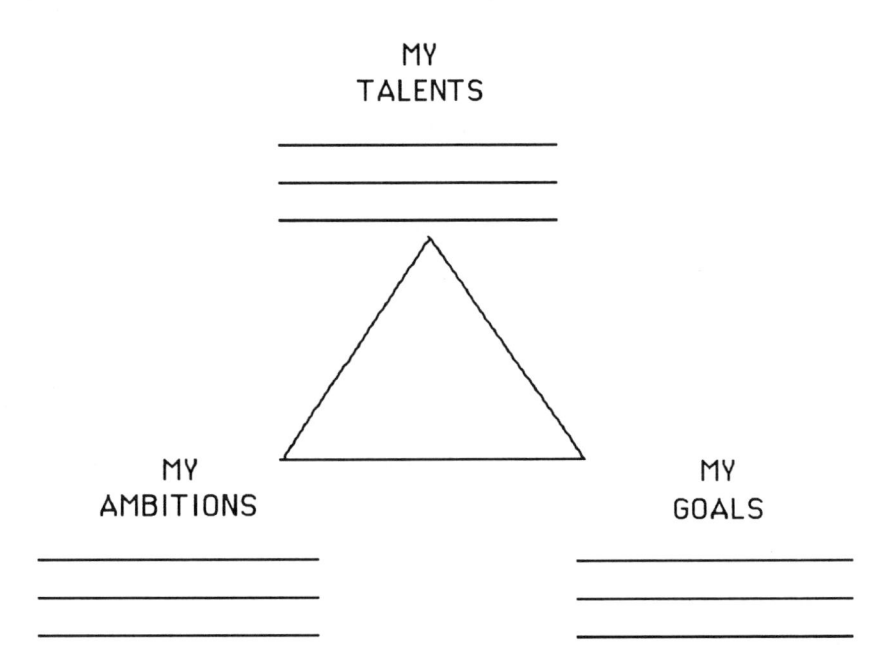

```
                    MY
                  TALENTS
                _____
                _____
                _____
                     /\
                    /  \
                   /    \
                  /      \
                 /        \
                /_____\
     MY                         MY
  AMBITIONS                    GOALS
_____              _____
_____              _____
_____              _____
```

According to self-psychology, the healthy self emerges as a result of *mirroring* from the empathic parent(s). If we are mirrored in a consistently unempathic manner, the result may be an inauthentic self.

After thoughtful reflection, are these really *your* talents, ambitions and goals, or are they based on expectations or definitions mirrored by others?

_____

_____

_____

_____

_____

_____

_____

8 Personal Workbook

9. **The Most Significant Events in My Life.** Make a timeline of your life. Along the line, identify the events that have impacted you most powerfully. These might include, but are not limited to, achievements, acquisitions, attachments, awakenings, failures, successes, separations, unions.

BIRTH   PRESENT

What do these events tell you about your decision to become a professional helper, and how might they influence your efficacy?

_____
_____
_____
_____
_____
_____
_____
_____
_____
_____
_____
_____
_____
_____
_____
_____
_____
_____
_____
_____

10. **What I read.** List the last ten books you have read. Once the list is completed, consider what it might tell you about where you look for instruction and what you value as *authority*.

1. _____
2. _____
3. _____
4. _____
5. _____
6. _____
7. _____
8. _____
9. _____
10. _____

_____
_____
_____
_____
_____
_____
_____
_____
_____
_____
_____
_____

Personal Workbook

11. **My Recent Movie History.** List the last five movies you have seen and review your emotional responses to these experiences. What characters did you identify with most; identify with least?

MOVIE	EMOTIONAL/IDENTIFICATION RESPONSES
1. _____	_____
2. _____	_____
3. _____	_____
4. _____	_____
5. _____	_____

12. **My Own Therapeutic History.** It has been said that a professional helper can only go as far with another as he or she has gone with self. Detail below your experience in your own therapy. What did you find most productive and least productive? What were your most helpful and least helpful therapists like? What did you struggle with most in therapy? If you have not been in therapy, what would cause you to be fearful and resistant to a process which you now say you want to pursue as a career?

13. **The House I Grew Up In.** Using crayons and your opposite hand (i.e., your left hand if you are right-handed or your right hand if you are left-handed, or your less preferred hand if you are ambidextrous) draw the house you grew up in.

Part 1   Who? What? and Why Now?   13

What was it like to come home to this house? Where was your room? What was it like? Did you share it with someone? If so, with whom? What secrets did this house contain?

_____
_____
_____
_____
_____
_____
_____
_____
_____
_____
_____
_____
_____
_____
_____
_____
_____
_____
_____
_____
_____
_____
_____
_____
_____
_____

14 Personal Workbook

If you could have placed a sign in the front yard telling passersby what was going on inside your house, what would it say?

14. **Your Family of Origin.** Using your opposite hand (i.e., your right hand if you are left-handed or your left hand if you are right-handed, or your less preferred hand if you are ambidextrous), draw in stick figures your family of origin. Place the children left to right in birth order from youngest to oldest. Refer to Adler (1958, pp. 144-155) for birth order discussion.

Think about your place in your family, and what implications it might have for your adult life, and your abilities and liabilities as a professional helper.

_____
_____
_____
_____
_____
_____
_____
_____
_____

16 Personal Workbook

15. **Boundaries.** Boundaries are essential to healthy functioning in all human relationships. This is especially underscored in the professional helping relationship.

    Think about your preferred style(s) of attachment (See Pistole, 1989) and consider what establishing and maintaining boundaries means to you.

A. **My House of Origin.** From your memory, draw the floor plan of the house you grew up in. Identify the places of privacy as well as the common areas shared by family members.

What rooms in the house were off limits to you? How were you informed of this, by whom, and what were the reasons given for this restriction?

Note the number and placement of bathrooms. If there was only one to be shared by all family members, how was the time-share negotiated to insure privacy for each family member?

B. **The Door to My Room.** Think about the room in the house that you grew up in that was designated as *yours*. Was it yours alone or did you share it with someone? If you did share it, who was that someone and what was the nature of your relationship with that person? Now, imagine the door below as the door to your room. Use crayons to color the door as you choose.

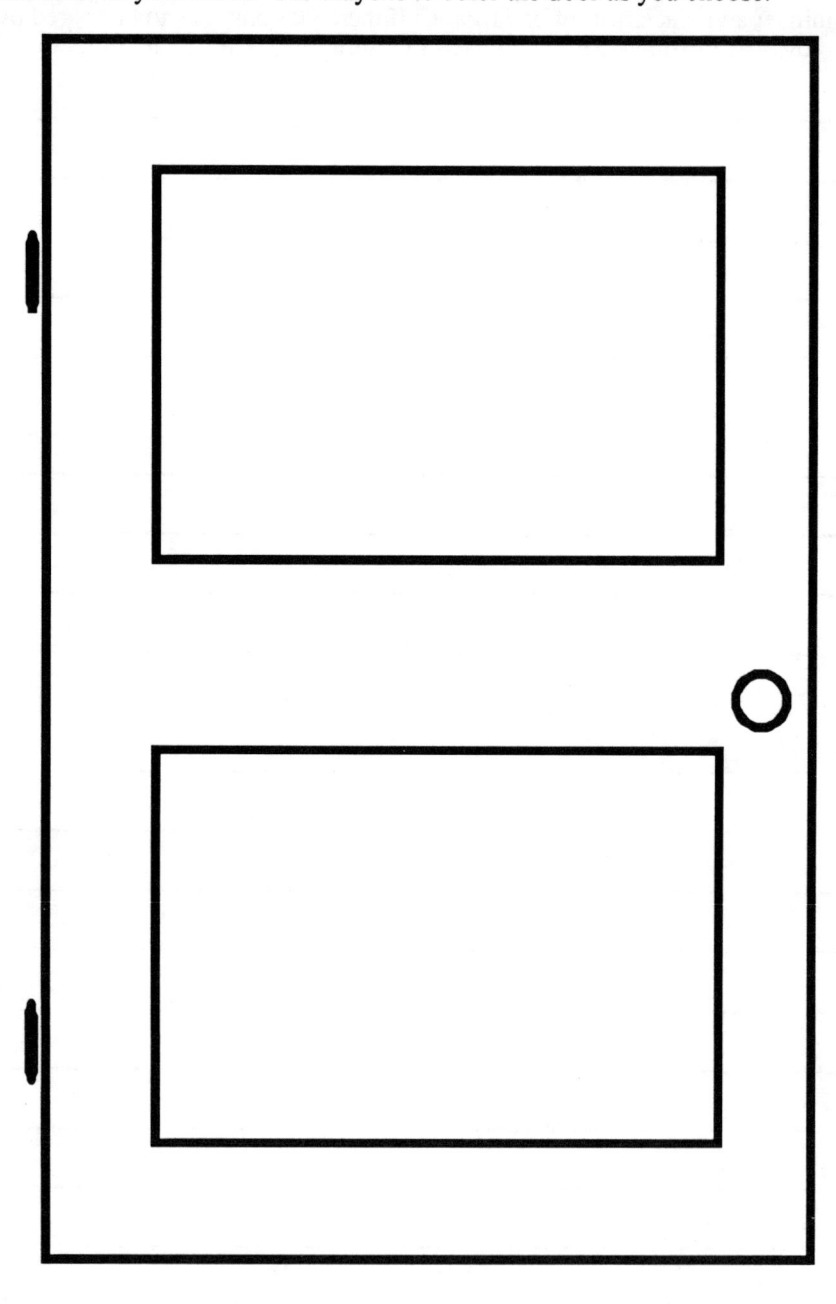

What might the color you have selected signify? Write on the door what you would say to alert others to stay away (e.g., "Keep Out," "Beware of Dog" or what one had to do to gain admission (e.g., "Please Knock"). Is it possible to lock the door? Does anyone else have the key? What kinds of feelings do you remember having inside the room? What might you have learned from the foregoing exercises about your own boundaries?

20   Personal Workbook

16. **My Top Five Teachers.** Go back across your educational experience from pre-school onward. Who are the teachers who remain in your mind as the most influential, either in a positive or negative sense? What was it about these teachers which gave them this place of prominence in your life?

	TEACHER'S NAME	INFLUENCE(S)
1.	_____	_____
2.	_____	_____
3.	_____	_____
4.	_____	_____
5.	_____	_____

When was the last time you spoke with each of these teachers? What was said?

_____

_____

_____

17. **My Favorite Childhood Story.** What remains in your mind as your favorite childhood story? Who passed it along to you? What about the story was so appealing? Was it read to you, did you read it, or was it given from an oral tradition? Which character(s) did you most identify with? How might this story relate to your present desire to become a professional helper?

18. **My Favorite Childhood Toys.** What toys from childhood do you remember as being your favorites? What was it about these toys that you found so engaging? Did you play with them alone or with others? Where are those toys now? How might they relate to your desire to become a professional helper?

_____
_____
_____
_____
_____
_____
_____
_____
_____
_____
_____
_____
_____
_____
_____
_____
_____
_____
_____
_____
_____
_____
_____
_____
_____

19. **What Makes Me Angry?** The counseling literature indicates that emerging counselors often have difficulty with so-called "negative affect." Alschuler & Alschuler (1984) have defined anger as "a temporary internal state in response to being hurt" (p. 26). It is to be understood that anger here is being differentiated from hostility and rage. List five things (events, experiences, traits, behaviors, people, groups) that cause you to feel anger. When you feel anger from particular experiences, what kind of hurt might it be defending?

	MAKES ME ANGRY	PERSONAL HURT
1.	_____	_____
2.	_____	_____
3.	_____	_____
4.	_____	_____
5.	_____	_____

How might what you have identified above impact your work as a professional helper? What kinds of people would be most likely to trigger your anger response? What might these images tell you about undeveloped parts of yourself? What could you do to prevent possible therapeutic failures from your predisposition to anger?

_____
_____
_____
_____
_____
_____
_____
_____
_____
_____
_____
_____
_____
_____

24   Personal Workbook

20. **How Do Others See Me?** Interview some of your frequent associates who can be relied upon to give you honest feedback. Ask what attracts them to you; what prevents them from getting closer to you; what they see when you are at your best; at your worst.

_____
_____
_____
_____
_____
_____
_____
_____
_____
_____
_____
_____
_____
_____
_____
_____
_____

21. **How Do I Re-Create Myself?** List below the five most effective ways you have fun and relax.

1. _____
2. _____
3. _____
4. _____
5. _____

22. **My Cultural Heritage.** Wrenn (1962) suggested the notion of cultural encapsulation and "the encapsulated counselor." This term refers to the clinician's inability to view the world of the client from the client's own perspective.

A. As honestly as you can, respond to the following questions.

What is your gender? _____

What is your sexual orientation? _____

List other traits you possess that have cultural implications (e.g., physical challenges).

_____
_____
_____
_____
_____
_____
_____

How would you describe your ethnicity of origin? _____

_____
_____

In what dominant culture(s) have you been socialized? _____

_____
_____
_____
_____

What was the size and nature of your family of origin? _____

_____
_____
_____
_____
_____
_____

Personal Workbook

Where were you in the birth order? _____
_____
_____

What language(s) was (were) spoken in your family? _____
_____
_____
_____

What was the emotional climate of your family of origin? _____
_____
_____
_____
_____
_____
_____

Who were the overt and covert leaders of your family system? _____
_____
_____
_____
_____
_____
_____

How were *male* and *female* defined in your family? _____
_____
_____
_____
_____
_____
_____

What roles were assigned to males and females in your family? _____

_____

_____

_____

_____

_____

_____

_____

What was the attitude toward sexuality and sex in your family? _____

_____

_____

_____

_____

_____

_____

_____

How was the identity of a particular individual formed within your family system (See Myers, et al., 1991)? _____

_____

_____

_____

_____

_____

_____

_____

_____

_____

Personal Workbook

What part did religion occupy within your family? _____

_____
_____
_____
_____
_____
_____

What was mealtime like in your family? _____

_____
_____
_____
_____
_____
_____

What were the predominant rituals in your family? _____

_____
_____
_____
_____
_____
_____

Who handled the money in your family? _____

_____
_____
_____

What was the music you listened to growing up? _____

_____

_____

_____

_____

Who were the revered artists in your culture of origin? _____

_____

_____

_____

_____

_____

_____

What were the stated and unstated expectations of this culture for its members?

_____

_____

_____

_____

_____

_____

How was death dealt with in this culture? _____

_____

_____

_____

_____

How were beauty and ugliness defined in this culture? _____

_____

_____

_____

_____

Personal Workbook

What part did food occupy in this culture? _____
_____
_____
_____
_____
_____
_____

What constituted physical attractiveness in this culture? _____
_____
_____
_____
_____
_____
_____

How was anger handled in this culture? _____
_____
_____
_____
_____
_____
_____
_____

What were the identified taboos of your culture of origin? _____
_____
_____
_____
_____
_____
_____
_____

How was *mental health* defined in your culture of origin? _____
_____
_____
_____
_____

What part did alcohol and other drugs occupy in your culture of origin? _____
_____
_____
_____
_____

Who were the heroes of your family of origin? _____
_____
_____
_____
_____
_____

How was discipline handled in your culture of origin? _____
_____
_____
_____
_____

How often did your family re-locate while you were growing up (e.g., neighborhood to neighborhood, town to town, state to state, country to country)? _____
_____
_____
_____
_____

32   Personal Workbook

B. **The Family Flags.** Create flags for both your family (culture) of origin and your current family. Use the sketches below to try out some ideas first, then transfer your ideas, using colored pencils, drawings, or pictures cut from newspapers or magazines, to large pieces of paper or fabric. These images are to symbolize what these cultures value and hold to be necessary for their membership.

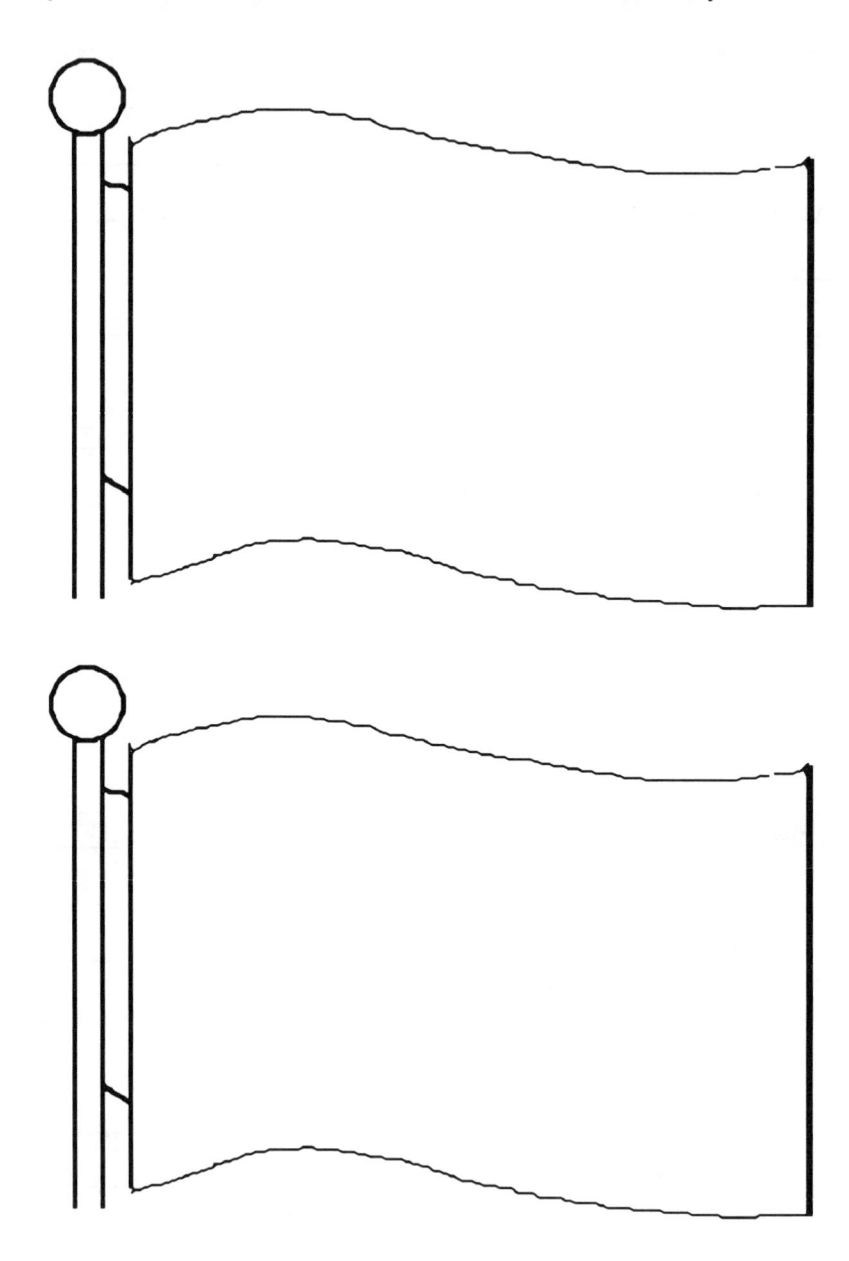

Once the flags are done, consider what they say and how they might come into conflict or find harmony with each other and with persons from differing cultures (i.e., persons who might come to you for counseling).

34 Personal Workbook

C. **Clients Come In Many Forms.** Consider the following descriptions of persons you might encounter in the counseling clinic. Based on the accrued impact of your own enculturation, indicate how you might initially respond to these persons.

Mark an "x" along the line indicating your most immediate response.

Rejection	Warm Acceptance	Fusion
no identification	*optimal identification*	*over identification*

----
middle-class female homemaker

----
right-wing anti-abortion activist

----
gay white male college freshman

African-American physician

----
domestic violence perpetrator

----
white female middle-aged alcoholic

----
convicted child abuser

----
accused child abuser

----
domestic violence victim

----
abused child

----
religious fundamentalist

----
lesbian mother

----
gay male AIDS victim

----
heterosexual female AIDS victim

Japanese-American female exchange student

_____ obese African-American female

_____ effeminate heterosexual male

_____ effeminate homosexual male

_____ masculine heterosexual female

_____ masculine homosexual female

_____ uneducated farm family

_____ left-wing anti-abortion activist

_____ Hispanic migrant worker

_____ wealthy Hispanic attorney

_____ Ku-Klux-Klan member

_____ gay rights activist

_____ militant anti-Christian activist

_____ orthodox Jewish rabbi

_____ gay male couple

_____ militant environmentalist

_____ strip-mining chief executive

_____ animal abuser

_____ welfare mother

_____
ten-year-old child born out of marriage

_____
convicted arsonist

_____
Islamic separatist

_____
lesbian female couple

_____
white male executive convicted of sexual harassment

_____
mother indicted for killing her two-year-old child

_____
African-American menopausal female

_____
adolescent male Puerto-Rican gang member

_____
white male drug dealer

_____
adolescent male gay basher

_____
white male alcoholic banker

_____
convicted male rapist

_____
Southern Baptist minister

_____
gay Catholic priest

_____
heterosexual pedophile gym teacher

_____
young white female junior league member

_____
elderly African-American Alzheimer's victim

_____
white male adolescent convicted of killing a police officer

Part 1 Who? What? and Why Now?

_____ teen-aged anorexic white female

_____ male counselor accused of client sexual abuse

_____ fifteen-year-old mother accused of throwing
her newborn child into a garbage dumpster

_____ forty-year-old white male going through mid-life crisis

_____

Based on how you have responded to the above, look for patterns of *no identification*, *optimal identification*, and *over identification*. How might these indicate the populations with which you are *most ready/least ready* to work?

_____

_____

_____

_____

_____

_____

_____

_____

_____

_____

_____

_____

_____

_____

_____

_____

Optimal Therapeutic Relationality

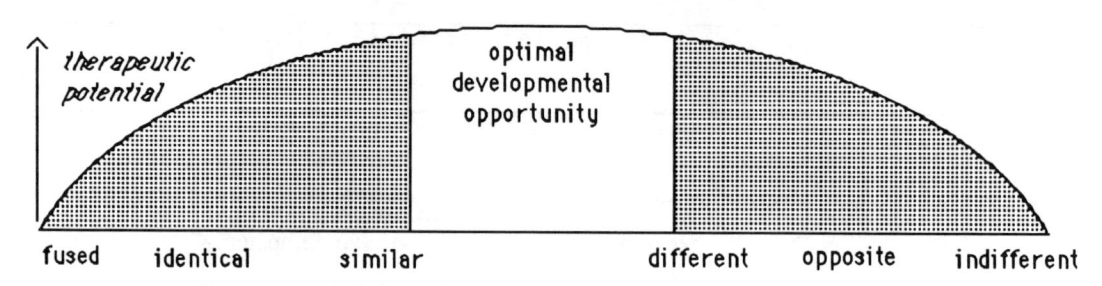

↑ therapeutic potential

fused — identical — similar — [optimal developmental opportunity] — different — opposite — indifferent

The professional helping relationship is best supported by optimal similarities and differences. Too far in either direction away from this space can impair therapeutic efficacy.

Think about the individuals listed in 22C above and consider where you would find yourself along this scale of relationship with each one.

_____
_____
_____
_____
_____
_____
_____
_____
_____
_____
_____
_____
_____
_____
_____
_____
_____
_____
_____

What are the dynamics of your own *enculturated* values that could cause you to be therapeutically impaired, either by *under*-identifying or *over*-identifying with particular populations? What might your resistance to these people be telling you about your own unresolved conflicts and issues? What might you do to overcome these barriers?

From the above list of potential clients, list three populations with which you now see yourself as *most likely* to be helpful as a therapist:

List three populations with which you now see yourself as *least likely* to be helpful. Consider how you would make arrangements to refer these persons to counselors who might be able to help them.

23. **Reality Is In the Eye of the Beholder.** Adapted from Gordon, D. (1988) and used by permission.

> The Sufis tell a story about a man who was walking down a strange road one day when he came upon a group of terrified villagers fleeing toward him. He stopped the panic-stricken mob to ask them what was the matter, and they cried that there was a monster in the fields. They pointed out to the field, but all the man saw was a watermelon. He turned back to the villagers and, scoffing and sneering, told the ignorant people that there was nothing there but a watermelon. When the villagers insisted that it was indeed a monster, the suddenly wary traveler accused them of lying. The enraged villagers fell upon the man and killed him for being a fool.
>
> A short while later, another, wiser man came down that same road, asked about the trouble, and, following the trembling fingers pointing out to the field, saw only the watermelon. The stranger drew his knife and, with a blood-curdling whoop, ran into the field, leapt upon the watermelon, and hacked it to bits. The villagers were so transported with joy over seeing their enemy destroyed that they made the stranger the leader of their village, a position he retained until it came to pass that he was able to teach them the difference between a monster and a watermelon (p. 164-165).

A. What significance does this story have for counselors-in-training?

B. List four "monsters" in your own life that others could see only as "watermelons:"

C. List four "watermelons" in your own life that others could see as "monsters:"

24. **Unfinished Business.** List below five people (more if necessary) with whom you have matters yet to be resolved.

What is the nature of these issues?

Now, write an uncensored letter to each of these persons, telling them how you really feel and stating your expectations. Mail the letters to yourself. How do you feel when you receive the letters? How might you work further toward resolving these issues with these persons?

25. **How Do I Come to Feel Safe?**

Trust is essential to the counseling process and clients will have to feel safe with you for any therapeutic progress to occur. For now, imagine a situation in which you feel completely safe.

_____
_____
_____
_____
_____
_____
_____
_____
_____
_____

How might you re-create a facsimile of the above scene for your clients?

_____
_____
_____
_____
_____
_____
_____
_____
_____
_____

Part 1   Who? What? and Why Now?   43

26. **Life-Space**.

The *life-space* comes from the branch of psychology known as field theory, as developed by Kurt Lewin. It is a graphic depiction of "the totality of effective *psychological* factors for a given person at a particular time" (Marx & Cronan-Hillix, 4th ed., 1987, p. 214). The system utilizes valences and vectors to depict the strength and direction of attraction toward or away from identified goals. The life-space below illustrates the situation of a person who wants to become a physician. (Marx & Cronan-Hillix, 1987, 4th Edition, p. 215).

```
P  = person                      c  = college
G  = goal                        m  = medical school
ce = college entrance exams      i  = internship
                                 pr = establishing a practice
```

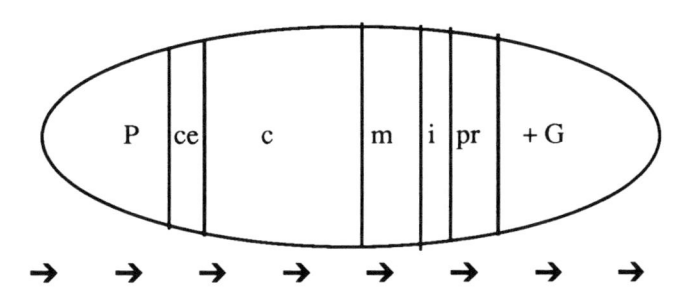

[Diagram: ellipse containing P | ce | c | m | i | pr | + G, with arrows pointing right below]

Notice that the goal bears a positive valence thus the vector is toward the goal. Between the person and the goal are identified barriers that may bear positive or negative valences, thus altering the direction of the vector.

Complete the life-space below for yourself with the goal of becoming a professional counselor. What kinds of barriers along the field might alter the direction of the vector? Examples might be getting a master's degree, the responsibilities of a family or other personal relationships, getting an internship, becoming licensed by a regulatory agency, setting up a practice, etc.). These will be personal to you and your life situation at this point in time.

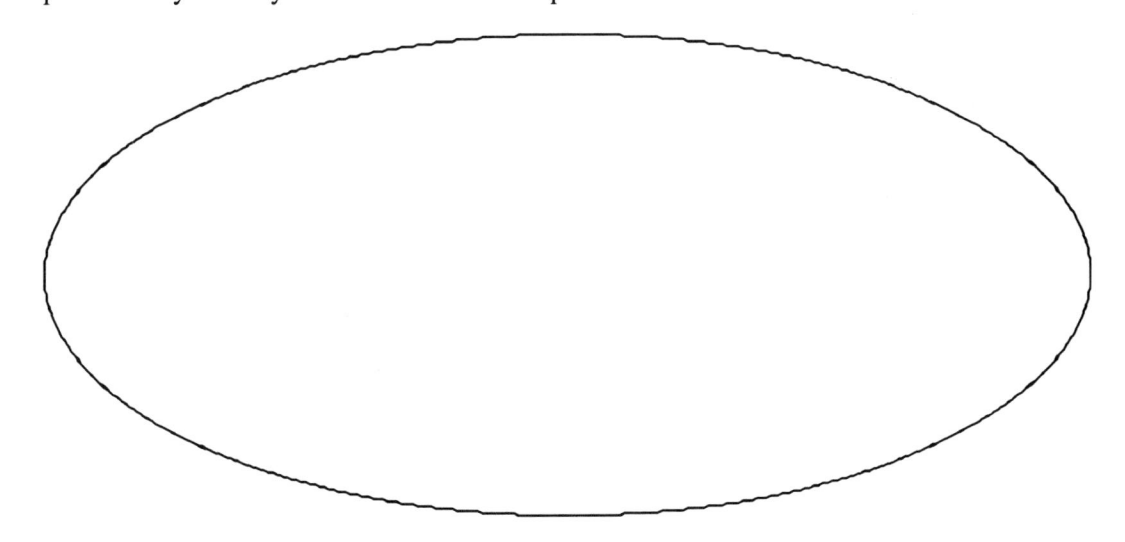

44 Personal Workbook

When you have finished the life-space, consider the strength (either positive or negative) of each barrier. If the vector is strong enough toward the goal, what kinds of negotiations will you have to effect with each barrier to reach the goal? If the negative strength of the combined barriers is equidistant to the positive valence of the goal, this would be indication of *ambi*-valence.

How might this exercise assist you in determining your level of resolve to realize your goal of becoming a professional counselor?

_____

_____

_____

_____

_____

_____

_____

_____

_____

_____

_____

_____

_____

_____

_____

_____

_____

_____

_____

_____

_____

_____

_____

27. **Personal Cycles.** Counseling necessitates the counselor being psychologically available to the counselee. This means that you must consider how you are typically throughout the day. For example, do you tend to be *matutinal* (given to morning activities) or *nocturnal* (given to evening activities)?

_____

_____

Consider the times of the day when you are typically at your best. What are the implications of this reality with regard to when you might see clients?

_____

_____

_____

_____

Do you typically consume a big lunch at noon? What are the possible consequences for your work with a one o'clock client?

_____

_____

Consider the following times and describe how you usually feel at these times.

    8:00 Monday morning _____

    6:30 Wednesday _____

    5:00 Tuesday afternoon _____

    12:00 noon on Monday _____

    4:30 Friday afternoon_____

    1:00 Thursday afternoon _____

    11:00 Thursday morning _____

    9:00 Monday following a holiday weekend_____

46 Personal Workbook

Now, suppose you had complete control over your schedule and could determine when you would deliver particular services. Consider the following and indicate on the clock how you would arrange this particular day.

MONDAY, THE 10TH OF MARCH

(1) 17-year-old HIV+ female client

(2) speaking engagement on community mental health with civic club

(3) 40-year-old male client going through a divorce

(4) breakfast

(5) lunch

(6) dinner

(7) supervision of graduate counseling student

(8) 22-year-old female client with career concerns

(9) facilitation of grief support group

(10) teaching a basic helping skills class at local community college

(11) time with your spouse, lover

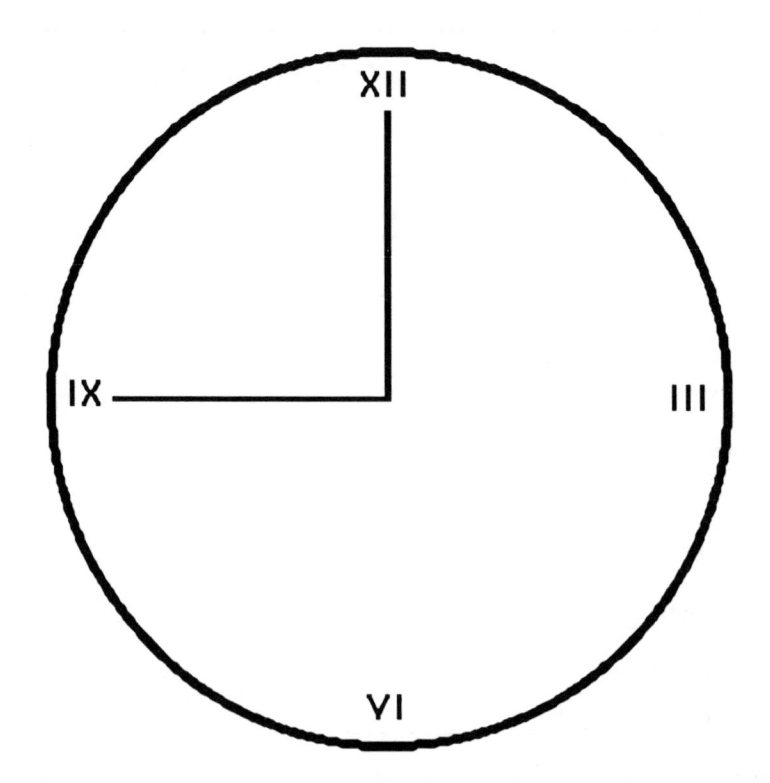

PART TWO

WHAT IS COUNSELING?

Garurira mbeu tiya kinya kimwe.
Change! Seeds are not kept in one gourd.
Gikuyu proverb (Jewell, 1993, p.17)

1. According to your textbook, "counseling involves an interpersonal relationship with someone who is actively seeking help with personal issues that interfere with or detract from a satisfactory life. The second person, the professional counselor, is willing to give help, personally capable of, and trained to help in a setting that permits help to be given and received" (p. 3).

    From your perspective, what do these terms mean?

    interpersonal relationship_____

    _____

    _____

    personal issues _____

    _____

    _____

    help_____

    _____

    _____

    trained_____

    _____

    _____

    setting_____

    _____

    _____

    What is changed about the counseling function when it is not voluntary (e.g., when a client is sent to counseling by the court)?

2. Counseling is often confused with other mental health enterprises such as:

> *guidance* - an advice-giving, information-providing activity often found in schools, colleges, and other academic settings
>
> *psychology* - the scientific-like study of human behavior founded in Leipzig, Germany in 1879 by Wilhelm Wundt
>
> *psychotherapy* - a more intrapsychic mental health function involving major personality change
>
> *psychiatry* - a branch of medicine dealing with organic brain function and the medication of the central nervous system
>
> *psychoanalysis* - a theory of personality and system of therapy founded by Sigmund Freud dealing with the contents of the unconscious mind and the bringing of that material to consciousness
>
> *social work* - a field that deals with social networks and strives to improve social conditions for members of a given community
>
> *consultation* - an ancillary counseling function in which a trained professional is engaged by another professional(s) to assess extant situations and make recommendations relative to work-related issues (Brown, Pryzwansky & Schulte, 1987).

According to Remley (1992), counseling is distinguished from any of the above in that it is based on prevention, early intervention, wellness, and empowerment. What do these terms mean to you?

prevention_____

_____

_____

_____

early intervention_____

_____

_____

_____

wellness_____

_____

_____

_____

empowerment_____

_____

_____

_____

Counseling can be further distinguished from other mental health enterprises in that it deals primarily with normal, relatively healthy individuals seeking to optimize their development and learn to negotiate their environments more effectively. Areas of concern that might be presented in counseling are:

- *relationships*
- *grief issues*
- *developmental transitions*
- *communication*
- *stress-related concerns*
- *parenting issues*
- *gender identity*

- *sexual dysfunction*
- *hopelessness*
- *career concerns*
- *anxiety*
- *issues of daily living*
- *family conflicts*
- *general life dissatisfaction*

Think about your emotional reactions to each of these issues and how these reactions might effect your ability to maintain the appropriate empathic relationship with clients. How healthy are you in these areas of life?

_____
_____
_____
_____
_____
_____
_____
_____
_____
_____
_____
_____
_____
_____
_____
_____
_____

3. The History of Mental Health-Related Disciplines.

QUICK QUIZ

_____ 1. Counseling is rooted primarily in:

    a. German mentalism
    b. American activism and social transition
    c. European intellectualism
    d. Eastern mysticism

_____ 2. The date of counseling's founding is:

    a. 1908
    b. 1879
    c. 1900
    d. 1938

_____ 3. The oft-recognized parent of the counseling profession is:

    a. Sigmund Freud
    b. Wilhelm Wundt
    c. Frank Parsons
    d. John B. Watson

_____ 4. Counseling has been influenced by:

    a. German structuralism
    b. American functionalism
    c. American individualism
    d. all of these

_____ 5. The birthplace of the counseling profession is:

    a. Leipzig, Germany
    b. Vienna, Austria
    c. Boston, Massachusetts
    d. Paris, France

_____ 6. The first counseling was:

    a. intrapsychic
    b. vocational
    c. interpersonal
    d. group

_____ 7. Counseling has been, and continues to be, influenced by:

    a. philosophy
    b. psychology
    c. economics
    d. education
    e. anthropology
    f. humanities
    g. all of these

_____ 8. Counseling's "identity" is:

    a. clear and easily articulated
    b. adolescent
    c. similar to that of physics
    d. emerging
    e. "a" & "c"
    f. "b" & "d"

_____ 9. Counseling is:

    a. a technology
    b. an art
    c. both of these
    d. neither of these

_____ 10. The *Zeitgeist* of the United States at the time of counseling's birth included:

    a. transition from an agrarian society to an industrial society
    b. strong anti-German sentiments
    c. transition from an industrial society to an information society
    d. fervent anti-intellectual religiosity

Answers: B, A, C, D, C, B, G, F, C, A

See Gummere (1988); Aubrey (1983).

4. **Is Counseling a Profession?** The term *profession* has a specific meaning. It was Abraham Flexner in 1915 who set forth the following conditions for a vocational activity to be recognized as a profession:

- *the objectives of professional work are definite and immediately practical*
- *educationally communicable techniques for the attainment of those objectives are available*
- *application of techniques involve essentially intellectual operations and practitioners exercise responsible discretion in matching techniques to individual problems*
- *the techniques are related to a systematic discipline, such as science, theology, or law, whose substance is large and complex, and hence ordinarily inaccessible to laymen*
- *members of the profession are organized in some kind of society, with rules for membership and exclusion based in part on professional competence*
- *the aims of the professional organization are at least in part altruistic rather than merely self-serving, and entail a code of ethics whose sanctions are also invoked, along with those of competence, in determining membership in the society and therefore legitimate practice of the profession*

Based on the above conditions, respond to the following questions with regard to counseling:

A. What are the stated objectives of counseling? _____

B. Are the techniques of counseling educationally communicable? _____

C. What about the fundamental operations of counseling such as compassion, empathy, positive regard which are not essentially intellectual? _____

D. Are the techniques of counseling matched to individual problems? What about cross-cultural considerations? _____

E. *So, is counseling a profession?* _____

52 Personal Workbook

5. **Professional Areas as Treatment of Choice.**

   Consider the following scenarios and indicate whether

   A. guidance

   B. psychology

   C. psychotherapy

   D. psychiatry

   E. psychoanalysis

   F. consultation

   G. social work

   H. counseling

   might be most readily indicated as the discipline of choice:

   _____ Mark is concerned about his apparent inability to establish satisfying interpersonal relationships.

   _____ Angie cannot decide whether to take Advanced Brain Physiology or Driver's Education.

   _____ Paul wants to take the MMPI.

   _____ José needs to be screened for severe depression and possible medication.

   _____ Laurie is suffering from obsessive-compulsive tendencies and wants to explore them intrapsychically.

   _____ James wants to explore his dreams.

   _____ Maria is having difficulty finding community resources for her three children.

   _____ Smith Corporation is experiencing excessive absenteeism among its employees.

   #Answers: H, A, B, D, C, E, G, F

6. **The *Weltanschauung* of a Profession and its Members.** Consider the following aspects of *worldview* and mark an X with a red pencil along the line where you perceive yourself operating in the world most frequently. Then using a black pencil, mark with an X where you see counseling as a profession operating most frequently:

---

structuralism   *functionalism*
(the contents of a thing)   (what a thing does)

---

determinism   *indeterminism*
(events explicable in terms of antecedents)   (events not explicable in terms of antecedents)

---

empiricism   *phenomenalism*
(truth is observable directly)   (truth is not directly observable)

---

quantitativism   *qualitativism*
(expressed in terms of counting and measuring)   (expressed in terms of essence)

---

individualism   *pluralism*
(emphasis on the individual)   (emphasis on the group)

---

deductivism   *inductivism*
(assessment begins with assumed truths)   (assessment begins without assumed truths)

---

purism   *eclecticism*
(adherence to a single body of knowledge)   (adherence to many bodies of knowledge)

---

objectivism   *subjectivism*
(emphasis on observer and the observed)   (emphasis on the observer as the observed)

---

linearity   *circularity*
(events and experiences seen as successive)   (events and experiences seen as reciprocal)

---

microscopic   *macroscopic*
(emphasis on smallest possible units)   (emphasis on larger relational view)

---

product   *process*
(emphasis on outcome)   (emphasis on contextually-defined movement)

---

cure   *healing*
(emphasis on eradication of toxic elements)   (integration and transformation of toxic elements)

historicism	*futurism*
(emphasis on events past)	(emphasis on events possibly to come)

staticism	*dynamism*
(things are stable)	(things are constantly in flux)

content	*context*
(the parts of the story)	(the subjective meanings of the parts of the story)

concretism	*ambiguity*
(specific, close-ended)	(non-specific, open-ended)

structured	*unstructured*
(clear, defined expectations)	(no clear, defined expectations)

elemental	*systemic*
(emphasis on the singular)	(emphasis on the plural and relational)

Based on the above, how do you see your current way of viewing and being in the world as related to your perception to the extant status of the counseling profession? Discuss this with your professor, other counseling professionals, your colleagues, and your therapist. (Adapted from Marx & Cronan-Hillix, 4th Edition, 1987, pp. 104-106).

_____
_____
_____
_____
_____
_____
_____
_____
_____
_____
_____
_____

Part 2 What Is Counseling? 55

7. **What the Counseling Profession Might Offer You as a Career.** Much is written about what it takes to become a professional counselor along with all that will be expected of you to earn that professional title. But what does a career as a professional counselor have to offer you in a practical sense? This *is* a reasonable question because counseling may become your livelihood and you have expectations and needs from a career, especially one that demands such dedication and preparation.

A. What will it take following the granting of your degree to become licensed as a professional counselor in your state of residence?

B. What is the market like in your area for professional counselors? the occupational outlook?

C. What annual income might a professional counselor expect to make? Consider both agency/institutional employment and private practice. How does counseling compare in terms of career opportunity with other mental health professions?

D. What are the liability costs (e.g., malpractice insurance, professional dues) that you will face?

E. What data are available to indicate the average career life expectancies of professional counselors? Why do persons leave the counseling profession?

56 Personal Workbook

Following is a roster of regulatory boards for professional counselors across the United States. Contact the agency in your state to help answer the above questions. In addition, you might interview some counselors in practice and find out about their career-related experiences.

Alabama
Board of Examiners in Counseling
P.O. Box 550397
Birmingham, AL 35255
205-933-8100
205-933-6700 (fax)

Arizona
Counselor Credentialing Committee of the Board of Behavioral Examiners
1645 W. Jefferson, Rm. 426
Phoenix, AZ 85007
602-542-1882
602-542-1830 (fax)

Arkansas
Board of Examiners in Counseling
Southern Arkansas University
P.O. Box 1396
Magnolia, AR 71753-5000
501-235-5149
501-234-1842 (fax)

California
Board of Behavioral Science Examiners
400 R Street, Suite 3150
Sacramento, CA 95814-6240
916-445-4933 (recorded info)
916-322-4910 (fax)

Colorado
Board of Licensed Professional Counselor Examiners
1560 Broadway, Suite 1340
Denver, CO 80202
303-894-7766
303-894-7790 (fax)

Delaware
Board of Professional Counselors of Mental Health
P.O. Box 1401
Cannon Bldg.
Dover, DE 19903
302-739-4522
302-739-2711 (fax)

District of Columbia
DC Board of Professional Counselors
605 G St., NW, Rm. 202, Lower Level
Washington, DC 20001
202-727-5365

Florida
Board of Clinical Social Workers, Marriage & Family Therapists, & Mental Health Counselors
Agency for Health Care Administration
1940 N. Monroe Street
Tallahassee, FL 32399-0753
904-487-2520
904-921-2569 (fax)

Georgia
Composite Board of Professional Counselors, Social Workers, and Marriage & Family Therapists
166 Pryor Street, SW
Atlanta, GA 30303
404-656-3933
404-651-9532 (fax)

Idaho
Idaho State Counselor Licensure Board
Bureau of Occupational Licenses
1109 Main Street, Suite 220
Boise, ID 83702-5642
208-334-3233
208-334-3945 (fax)

Illinois
Professional Counselor Licensing & Disciplinary Board
320 West Washington
Springfield, IL 62786
217-785-0872
217-782-7645 (fax)

Iowa
Iowa Behavioral Science Board
4th Floor, Lucas Building
Des Moines, IA 50319
515-242-5937 or 291-6352
515-281-4958 (fax)

Kansas
Behavioral Science Regulatory Board
712 S. Kansas Avenue
Topeka, KS 66603-3817
913-296-3240
913-296-3112 (fax)

Louisiana
Licensed Professional Counselors Board of Examiners
4664 Jamestown Avenue, Suite 125
Baton Rouge, LA 70808-3218
504-922-1499
504-922-2160 (fax)

Maine
Board of Counseling Professionals
State House
Station #35
Augusta, ME 04333
207-582-8723
207-624-8637 (fax)

Maryland
Board of Examiners of Professional Counselors
Metro Executive Center, 3rd Floor
4201 Patterson Avenue
Baltimore, MD 21215-2299
410-764-4732
410-764-5987 (fax)

Massachusetts
Board of Allied Mental Health & Human Service Professionals
100 Cambridge Street, 15th Floor
Boston, MA 02202
617-727-1716
617-727-2197 (fax)

Michigan
Michigan Board of Counseling
P.O. Box 30018
Lansing, MI 48909
517-335-0918 (applications)
517-335-3596 (fax)

Mississippi
Miss. Board of Examiners of LPCs
P.O. Drawer 3814
Mississippi State, MS 39762-6239
601-325-3426
601-325-3263 (fax)

Missouri
Missouri Committee for Professional Counselors
3605 Missouri Blvd.
Box 1335
Jefferson City, MO 65102-1335
314-751-0018
314-751-4176 (fax)

Montana
Board of Social Work Examiners &
  Professional Counselors
Arcade Bldg., Lower Level
111 North Jackson
P.O. Box 200513
Helena, MT 59620-0513
406-444-4285
406-444-1667 (fax)

Nebraska
Board of Examiners in Professional
  Counseling
Bureau of Examining Boards
301 Centennial Mall South
P.O. Box 95007
Lincoln, NE 68509-5007
402-471-2115
402-471-0380 (fax)

New Hampshire
NH Board of Examiners of Psych. and
  Mental Health Practice
105 Pleasant St.
Concord, NH 03301
603-271-6762

New Jersey
New Jersey Professional Counselor
  Examiners Committee
Division of Consumer Affairs
P.O. Box 45033
Newark, NJ 07101
908-232-3638

New Mexico
Counselor Therapy & Practice Board
P.O. Box 25101
Santa Fe, NM 87504
505-827-7554
505-827-7560 (fax)

North Carolina
NC Board of Licensed Professional
  Counselors
P.O. Box 21005
Raleigh, NC 27619-1005
919-787-1980
919-571-8672 (fax)

North Dakota
ND Board of Counselor Examiners
P.O. Box 2735
Bismark, ND 58502
701-22408234

Ohio
Counselor & Social Work Board
77 South High Street
16th Floor
Columbus, OH 43266-0340
614-752-5161
614-644-0222 (fax)

Oklahoma
Licensed Professional Counselors
Licensed Marital & Family Therapists
1000 NE 10th Street
Oklahoma, OK 73117-1299
405-271-6030
405-271-1011 (fax)

Oregon
Board of Licensed Professional
  Counselors & Therapists
3218 Pringle Rd., SE #160
Salem, OR 97302-6312
503-378-5499

Rhode Island
Boards of Mental Health Counselors &
  M&F Therapists
Division of Professional Regulation
3 Capitol Hill
Cannon Bldg., Room 104
Providence, RI 02908-5097
401-277-2827
401-277-1272 (fax)

South Carolina
SC Dept. of LLR, Division of POL
Board of Examiners for LPC, AC, and
  MFT
P.O. Box 1115
Pierre, SD 57501
605-224-6281
605-224-6060 (fax)

Tennessee
State Board of Professional Counselors
  & M&F Therapists
282 Plus Park Blvd.
Nashville, TN 37247-1010
615-367-6249
615-367-6210 (fax)

Texas
Board of Examiners of Professional
  Counselors
1100 W. 49th Street
Austin, TX 78756-3183
512-834-6658
512-834-6677 (fax)

Utah
Division of Occupational &
  Professional Licensing
160 East 300 South
Salt Lake City, UT 84111
801-530-6597

Vermont
CCMHC Advisory Board
Office of Professional Regulation
109 State Street
Montpelier, VT 05609-1106
1-800-439-8683 (in Vermont)
802-828-2390
802-828-2496 (fax)

Virginia
Board of Professional Counselors
Dept. of Health Professions
6606 W. Broad St., 4th Floor
Richmond, VA 23230-1717
804-662-9912
804-662-9943 (fax)

Washington
Counselor Programs
Dept. of Health
Professional Licensing Services
  Division
P.O. Box 47869
Olympia, WA 98504-7869
360-664-9098
360-586-7774 (fax)

Wisconsin
Examining Board of Social Workers,
  M&F Therapists, & Professional
  Counselors
Dept. of Regulations & Licensing
1400 E. Washington Avenue
P.O. Box 8935
Madison, WI 53708-8935
608-267-7212
608-267-0644 (fax)

Wyoming
Mental Health Professions Licensing
  Board
2301 Central Avenue
Barret Bldg., 3rd Floor
Cheyenne, WY 82002
307-777-7788
307-777-6005 (fax)

58   Personal Workbook

8. **Toward Professional Status**. Membership in a profession involves not only competent and ethical practice of that profession, but also genuine effort on the part of the member to advance the profession. You will be called upon to be an active participant in your national and state professional organizations. What would this kind of involvement mean to you and your significant others in terms of money and time?

_____

_____

_____

_____

_____

_____

_____

_____

_____

_____

The primary professional organization of the counseling profession is the American Counseling Association (ACA). While the awarding of your degree in counseling will mark the first definitive element of your professional status, you can become involved *now* in the activities of the profession in which you are seeking status.

Join the American Counseling Association. As a student, you may qualify for a special membership rate. You can reach ACA headquarters by contacting

> ACA Public Affairs Department
> 5999 Stevenson Avenue
> Alexandria, Virginia 22304-3300
>
> 1-800-347-6647 (weekdays 8:30 a.m. - 7:30 p.m.)

Get Connected. Join the *International Counselors Network* on the Internet. Subscribe to

listserv@utkvm1.utk.edu OR listserv@utkvm1.bitnet

Through this discussion group, you can join in on conversations about many topics of interest to counselors. Also, check out the World Wide Web homepage produced by Doug Harris of the University of Arkansas: *Internet Resources for Counselors*. Point your Web Browser to

http://www.uark.edu/depts/cned/web/counsel.html

There are links to many Internet sites that may be of interest to you.

9. **What is Supervision?** Counseling is both a technology and an art. Your professional preparation will necessarily involve academic *and* experiential activities. Therefore, in addition to your classroom instruction, your program of studies will also include some type of praxis setting in which you will work with a client under the overview of a trained professional. This person is your *supervisor* and your relationship with that person is critical to your optimal professional development.

Bordin (1983) has identified and described the "supervisory working alliance." This term encompasses the relationship between the supervisor/supervisee as well as the tasks of the enterprise.

According to Bordin's model of supervision, the following goals are supported by the supervisory working alliance:

- *Mastery of specific skills.*
- *Enlarging one's understanding of clients.*
- *Enlarging one's awareness of process issues.*
- *Increasing awareness of self and impact on process.*
- *Overcoming personal and intellectual obstacles toward learning and mastery.*
- *Deepening one's understanding of concepts and theory.*
- *Providing a stimulus to research.*
- *Maintenance of standards of service.*

How might you seek to meet these goals with your supervisor in the early stages of your career?

10. **Essential Therapeutic Values.** Counseling is *not* a value-free activity. However, its values have been carefully established to provide an opportunity for persons to realize contextually defined optimal human development.

Strupp (1980) has set forth six (6) essential therapeutic values. While he is referring to psychotherapy, the same are applicable to counseling. These values are:

- *People have the right to personal freedom and independence.*

- *As adult members of a particular society, they have rights and privileges but they also have responsibilities toward others.*

- *To the greatest extent possible, people should be responsible for conducting their own lives, without undue dependence on others.*

- *People are responsible for their actions but not their feelings, fantasies, etc.*

- *People's individuality should be fully respected, and they should not be controlled, dominated, manipulated, coerced, or indoctrinated.*

- *People are entitled to make their own mistakes and to learn from their life experiences.*

Consider these values and place each alongside the personal values you bring to the counseling profession. Discuss this with your professor, your colleagues, and your therapist.

11. **Statement of Intent.** Most likely the admission process to your current program of studies required some type of statement as to what you intend to do with a degree in professional counseling. If it did not, write such a declaration of intent in the space below. If it did, write it again, now that you have been admitted to study. Has anything changed?

In your statement, answer these questions:

- *What do you hope to accomplish in your work as a counselor?*
- *Given your potentials and limitations, with what populations do you intend to work?*
- *How many people do you hope to help?*
- *What will you define as success/failure as a professional counselor?*

PART THREE

STAGES AND SKILLS OF COUNSELING?

These fellow mortals, every one, must be accepted as they are.
George Eliot
Adam Bede, ch. 17

1. **Social Relationship versus Professional (Helping) Relationship.** Counseling is an interpersonal human relationship. However, it is a *professional* relationship as opposed to a *social* relationship. It exists within a defined framework whereas social relationships exist within numerous settings and vary widely as to their nature and evolution.

   First, consider your social relationships. List below the ten (10) most significant social relationships (other than family) in which you are presently involved. How did each relationship come to be? Look for themes among these relationships? Do you primarily give or receive in each? Or, is the giving and receiving more or less mutual? Are each person's needs clearly stated in each relationship? How satisfying is each relationship?

   (1) J. Wu – Neighbor, kids same age, giving receiving mutual.

   (2) A. Chan – same

   (3) R. Rong – met thru church; Like a big sister; giving receiving mutual

   (4) E. Olivar – met in church. Talk about faith & family.

   (5) J. Lin – Volunteer also at TCCS. Facilitating parenting group. Very dependable.

   (6) a. Chen – calls for advice on parenting.

   (7) S. Yeh –

   (8)

   (9)

   (10)

64   Personal Workbook

2. **Elements of a Professional (Helping) Relationship.** The professional relationship is structurally defined and communicated:

> The professional relationship is *intentional*.
>
> The professional relationship is *confidential*.
>
> The professional relationship is *time-limited*.
>
> The professional relationship is for a *fee*.

A. While all relationships have some sort of structure, is the structure of your social relationships clearly defined and communicated at the beginning of the relationship? Does the structure tend to change as the social relationship proceeds? Is the purpose of the social relationship defined and made clear to all parties concerned at the onset? Are boundaries always clearly established? Do you and your friends discuss goals for the relationship? Do you meet with your friends for a specific time span to be applied to each meeting? Do you have some idea of a time when the friendship will end? Is each role for each person in the friendship discussed ahead of time or do they just seem to evolve as time passes?

Compare the implicit structure of the social relationship to the explicit structure of the professional (helping) relationship.

B. When you meet with your friends, how intentional is your behavior and theirs? Do you know *why* you are saying everything you say? Do you establish strategies for the outcome of the friendship?

C. How confidential are your friendships? Is confidentiality discussed as to its place and provisions in the friendship?

D. Do you charge your friends money for the time they spend with you and do you pay them for your time with them? Is it always clear and stated as to what you are getting from your friends and what they are getting from you?

_____

_____

_____

_____

_____

_____

_____

_____

3. **The Helping Crucible.** *The Random House Dictionary of the English Language*, 2d ed., unabridged (1987), defines a *crucible* as "a container ... employed for heating substances to high temperatures," and "a severe, searching test or trial."

   Counseling involves change and transformation. In order for the elements of change to undergo transformation, there must be a strong container. We'll call this concept *the helping crucible*. Its elements are:

A. Defined and Communicated Structure

   (1) counseling setting designed for help to be given and received

   (2) roles and boundaries clearly established

   (3) time-limited

B. Intentionality

   (1) begins with informed consent

   (2) mutually agreed-upon outcome goals

   (3) counselor-created process goals

   (4) sound and culturally appropriate interventions

C. Confidentiality

   (1) counselor commitment to client privacy

   (2) possible exceptions

   (3) existence or non-existence of privileged communication

D. Fee-Based

   (1) the only need of the counselor that is to be met in the helping relationship

   (2) consistent with the popular notion that "you get what you pay for"

   (3) concrete evidence of client's commitment to and investment in the helping process

Personal Workbook

Here, crucible is taken as a metaphor for the vessel (container) that holds the elements of the helping relationship and provides the necessary structure for therapeutic transformation to occur. It looks like this:

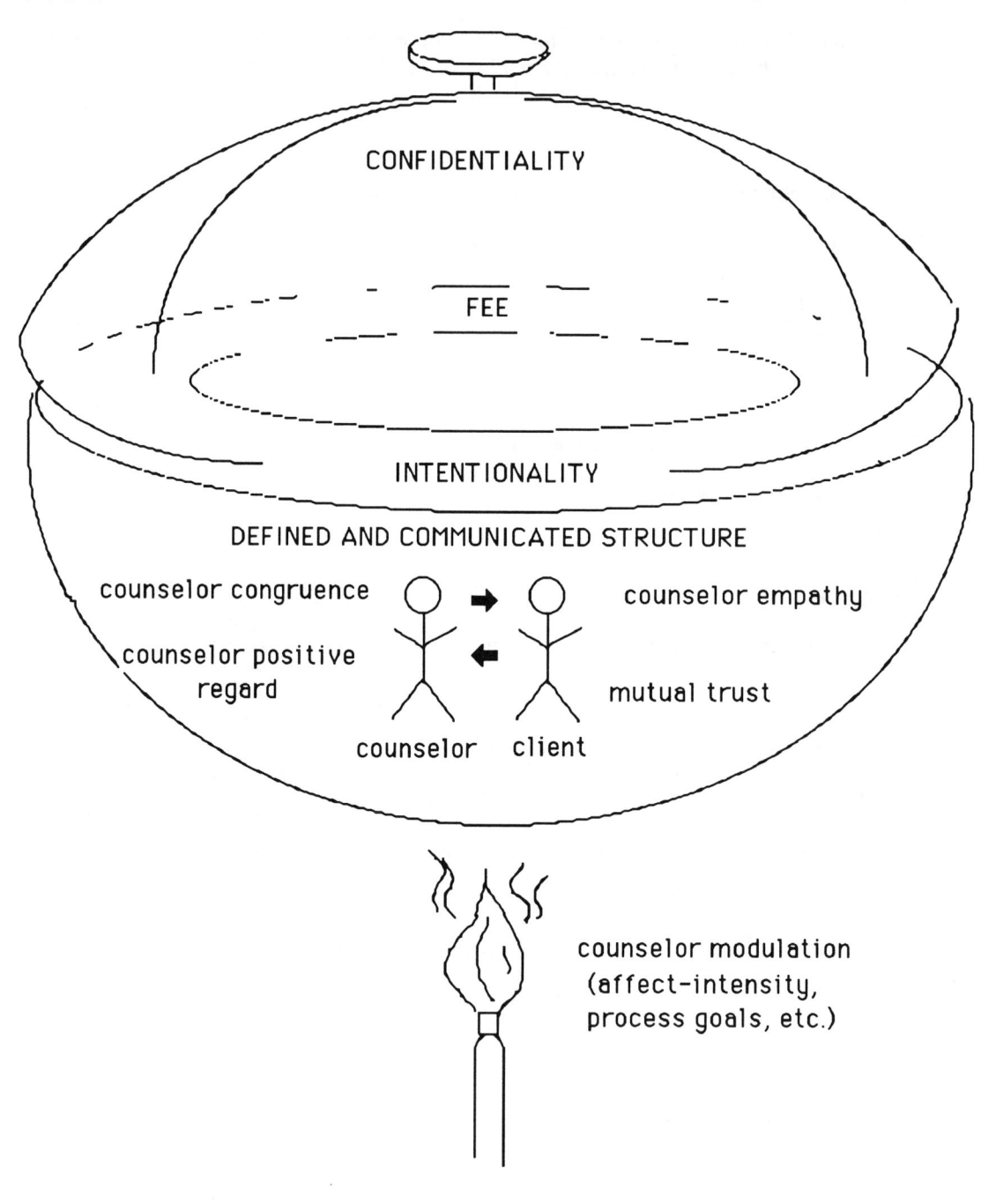

CONFIDENTIALITY

FEE

INTENTIONALITY

DEFINED AND COMMUNICATED STRUCTURE

counselor congruence → counselor empathy

counselor positive regard ← mutual trust

counselor   client

counselor modulation (affect-intensity, process goals, etc.)

Like any transformative process, certain conditions must exist within the container in order for the reaction to proceed. Inside the helping crucible, the following are considered core conditions:

- *mutual trust* - a function of safety
- *counselor positive regard* - a function of prizing
- *counselor empathy and its communication to the client* - a function of perspective-taking
- *counselor congruence* - a function of genuineness

(See Rogers, 1957).

Consider how both client and counselor might be impacted by the heat, intensity, and other prevailing conditions of the helping crucible.

Let's consider each element of the helping crucible in more detail.

A. **Defined and Communicated Structure**

(1) **The Setting**. Frank (1976) has suggested that persons who seek help are more likely to be helped *if they believe in the ability of the helper to help*. This premise could be applied to psychiatrists, witch doctors, faith healers, *and counselors*.

According to Brickman, et al (1982), the helping professions have been greatly influenced by the medical model in which the helping potential is invested in so-called *experts*. Consider the helping setting and what it might communicate to the client with regard to your expertise.

On the next page is an empty room. Sketch in how you would furnish it for the "dream setting" in which you will someday conduct your professional work. If you like, transfer your ideas to a larger piece of paper.

What kind of floor covering would you select? What color? What kind of lighting would you select - overhead, indirect, table lamps, candles? What about wallcovering - paper, paint, paneling? What colors - pastels, primary colors, combinations?

What kind of furniture would you choose? What style; what period? What would it be made of? How would it be upholstered? What colors would you select? What would these selections intend to communicate? How would the furniture be arranged (i.e., face to face, perpendicular, or at an angle)? What would this arrangement intend to communicate?

What kinds of books would fill the shelves? What would these volumes say about your philosophical-theoretical orientation; special areas of professional emphasis? With what would you line the walls - diplomas, license certificates, special achievements, art, photographs (spouse, children, lover, pets, parents, travel experiences)? What might these images communicate to the client about who you are? What kinds of objects (trinkets, statuary, pottery) would decorate the room? Where is the clock placed? Are there windows? Would the windows be covered? If so, with what? What about plants, fish tank, etc.?

What would be held inside closed cabinets that your client would not see (e.g., client records, personal correspondence, checkbook)?

How might meeting in the same setting each time over the course of the helping process, by way of consistency, contribute to the client's feeling of safety with the counselor?

_____

_____

_____

_____

_____

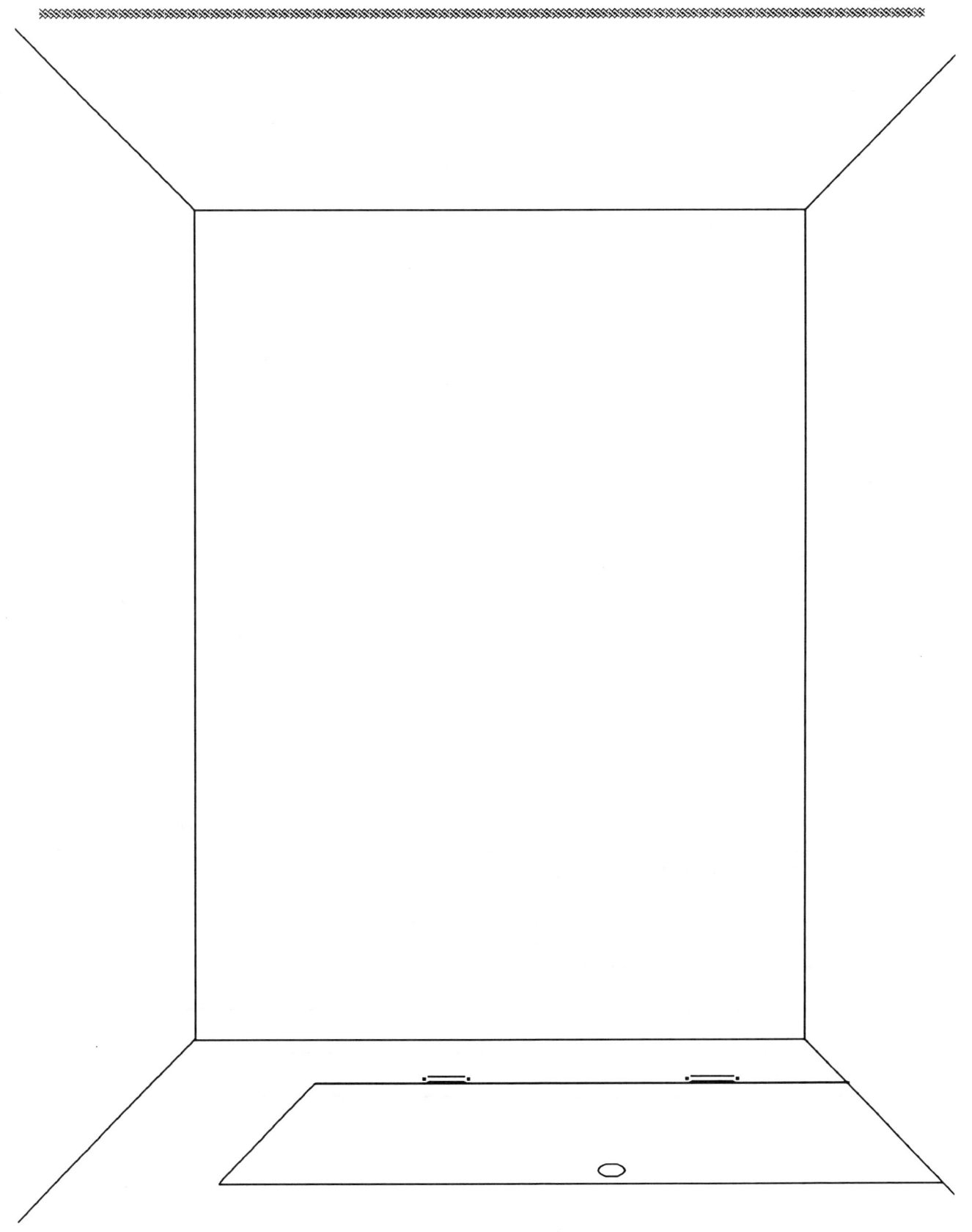

(2) **Assigned and Understood Roles**.

State the role of the professional counselor as you understand it. Name specific counselor responsibilities

_____

_____

_____

_____

_____

_____

State the role of the client as you understand it. Name specific client responsibilities

_____

_____

_____

_____

_____

_____

(3) **Time**. How does the Western conception of time contribute to the maintenance of the helping crucible? Consider the safety communicated by the *fifty-minute hour* or the *sixty-minute hour*. How might this time allotment need to be shortened for clients with limited attention span (e.g., children, adolescents) or perhaps extended for groups?

_____

_____

_____

_____

_____

_____

What if the client was not advised as to when the session with the counselor would end? How might this contribute to the client's feeling unsafe? How might a client be less willing to encounter painful material not knowing that the session will end at a stated time?

_____

_____

_____

_____

_____

_____

_____

What are the possible consequences when the counselor goes over time and does not end the session *as stated* at the beginning? Consider the parent who makes a statement to a child and then does not follow through. How might this lead to client mistrust of the counselor?

_____

_____

_____

_____

_____

_____

_____

How might the counselor's going over time in the session be a consequence of his or her countertransference?

_____

_____

_____

_____

_____

_____

_____

Personal Workbook

How would established and enforced time limits enhance the *value* of the time with the counselor in the client's mind?

_____

_____

_____

_____

_____

How might time limits enhance the counselor's attending to the client?

_____

_____

_____

_____

_____

While it is not possible to know exactly how long the helping process will take, consider the value of committing with a particular client for a stated number of sessions and then re-evaluating how well the process is working at that time. Compare this to an open-ended approach in which the client has no marker point to be working toward. How might this cause the client not to use the time in counseling wisely? *Consider how you would live your life differently if you did not know that you will, at some point, die.*

_____

_____

_____

_____

_____

B. **Intentionality**.

(1) **Informed Consent**. We live in a market economy. In counseling, the client is the consumer and has a right to know what counseling is about *prior* to engaging the process. This gains even more importance if you consider the mystery surrounding the mental health professions in the minds of the lay community.

Elements of informed consent:

- *the definition and purpose of counseling*
- *the theoretical orientation of the counselor*
- *the cost of the services*
- *the responsibilities of the counselor TO (not for) the client*
- *the responsibilities of the client*
- *the boundaries and singular relationship of the counselor and client*
- *confidentiality and its possible exceptions*
- *the existence or non-existence of privileged communication*
- *the time established for individual sessions as well as predicted duration of the helping process*
- *possible benefits to be accrued from the counseling process*
- *possible risks associated with the helping process*
- *outcome criteria to determine whether or not counseling has been successful*

How might these elements differ in meaning across cultures?

_____
_____
_____
_____
_____
_____
_____
_____

74 Personal Workbook

(2) **Outcome Goals.** How is this concept defined by your textbook?

_____

_____

_____

_____

_____

_____

_____

Counseling is NOT problem-solving. What might be meant by the word *problem*, beyond its popular connotation (i.e., something to be solved)?

_____

_____

_____

_____

_____

_____

Consider *problem* as: *concern, question, reason for seeking counseling, stressors, life conditions.*

How does *solution* differ from *resolution* (i.e., *re*-solution)?

_____

_____

_____

_____

_____

_____

Part 3   Stages and Skills of Counseling   75

How might a so-called solution rob the client of an opportunity to grow from mistakes?

___

How might a presenting problem evolve to reveal an underlying or secondary problem?

___

Consider Conrad in the movie *Ordinary People* (1980). Conrad went to see Dr. Berger and identified his "problem" as wanting to be more in control. Later in the work it became evident that Conrad was suffering from unresolved grief. How might the "need for control" be functionally related to powerful latent feelings associated with grief?

___

76   Personal Workbook

(3)   **Process Goals**. How is this concept defined by your textbook?

_____

_____

(4)   **Strategies and Interventions**. How do the authors of your textbook differentiate between a strategy and an intervention?

_____

_____

3.   **Confidentiality**. According to Corey, Corey, & Callanan (1993), confidentiality is defined as "the ethical and legal responsibility of mental-health professionals to safeguard clients from unauthorized disclosures of information given in the therapeutic relationship" (p. 102).

Quoted in the same source, Siegel (1979, p. 251) defines *privacy* as "the freedom of individuals to choose for themselves the time and the circumstances under which and the extent to which their beliefs, behavior, and opinions are to be shared [with] or withheld from others" (p. 103). *Privileged communication*, on the other hand, is quoted as being, according to Leslie (1991) "a *legal* concept protecting the right of clients to withhold testimony in a court proceeding" (p. 103). What are the exceptions to confidentiality as stated in informed consent? Does your state afford privileged communication to counselors? How might these factors influence the trust level of the client in counseling? Imagine how you might communicate differently these realities via *informed consent* to the following four clients:

Mexican-American female_____

_____

_____

Caucasian male involved in child custody suit with spouse _____

_____

_____

Accused domestic violence perpetrator _____

_____

_____

11-year-old child _____

_____

_____

D. **Fee-Based.**

  (1)　How do you attribute the value of that which you receive to what you pay for with money?

  (2)　What statement does a fee make to the client as consumer?

  (3)　How might the fee indicate concretely the client's investment in the helping process?

  _____
  _____
  _____
  _____
  _____
  _____

4. **Hearing versus Listening.** According to *Statistical Abstract of the United States* (1995, p. 140), there are more than 234,000,000 people in the United States free of any hearing impairment. If so many people experience no difficulty in hearing, why do so many people come to counseling and report feeling that they have never been heard? Perhaps this is because hearing is different from listening.

   Hearing is a *physiological* process. It involves the external ear into which vibrations are collected. These waves are passed to the inner ear. From here the signals are sent to the brain where associations are made with familiar patterns. This is what we call *hearing*.

   If you are a hearing individual, sit very still right where you are and record all the sounds you are hearing.

   _____
   _____
   _____
   _____
   _____
   _____
   _____
   _____

Personal Workbook

Listening is a *psychological* process. It involves cognitions, affects, body sensations, philosophical associations, compassion, and what Gendlin (1962) has described as "experiencing" or "felt-level experience."

Return to the sounds you are hearing right now. As you hear each one, what kinds of thoughts, feelings, beliefs, assumptions arise for you? For example, if you are hearing a siren from an emergency vehicle, what do you think, feel, and assume? Does the mind tell you, "someone is in trouble" or does it tell you that "help is on the way?"

5. **Content versus Context**.

> *"What is as important as knowledge?" asked the mind.*
> *"Seeing with the heart." answered the soul.*
>
> *Anonymous*

The *Random House Dictionary of the English Language,* 2d ed. unabridged. (1987) defines *content* as: "subjects or topics covered in a book or document." It defines *context* as: "the set of circumstances or facts that surround a particular event, situation, etc.

Consider the following case example:

> 23-year-old Angie goes to a university counseling center and tells the counselor that she is distressed over the fact that her father has taken away her American Express Card® and that she will now have to eat in the university dining center instead of out in the community at better restaurants. The counselor, a graduate trainee serving an internship went to her supervisor and informed him of the case. She somewhat sarcastically stated that *she* should be faced with such an "overwhelming problem." However, as they listened to the audio tape of the session with the young woman the supervisor heard in the client's voice an urgency and anxiety that would suggest more than reflected simply by the content of the client's story. He suggested that at the next session the counselor explore some of the affect associated with the client's story. It soon became evident that the young woman had suspicions that her parents' troubled marriage was about to end and that her father's removal of the credit card was a signal that the break-up was imminent. This was precisely the case. Consider how the counselor is called upon not only to pay attention to the content of a client's story, but also to the subjective meaning that the content holds for that client.

6. **Stages and Skills Elaborated.**

> *It's not the pot that grows the flower....*
> *(Romanovsky & Phillips, 1989)*

A. **By the way, what is a stage?** According to Shipley (1945), the etymology of the term *stage* presents the image of a tank, from the Latin *stagnum*, a pool (i.e., standing as opposed to running water)" (p. 349); the same root from which we get the word *stagnate*. Consider the implications of this word's history. Imagine a stage as an enclosure in which an individual's process is held and protected. Also imagine what could happen if the individual's process is imprisoned and detained from resuming its developmental course.

```
┌─────────────────────────────────┐
│                                 │
│                                 │
│           STAGE I               │
│                                 │
│    RAPPORT AND RELATIONSHIP     │
│                                 │
│                                 │
└─────────────────────────────────┘
```

Identify the elements of this container necessary to the process of counseling?

_____
_____
_____
_____
_____
_____
_____
_____

Part 3   Stages and Skills of Counseling   **81**

Another way to imagine the term *stage* is a raised platform from which a particular script is acted out. Imagine a stage as a designated space from which an individual acts out a particular developmental scenario. Also imagine what could happen if the counselor is merely a spectator and only vicariously involved in the client's drama?

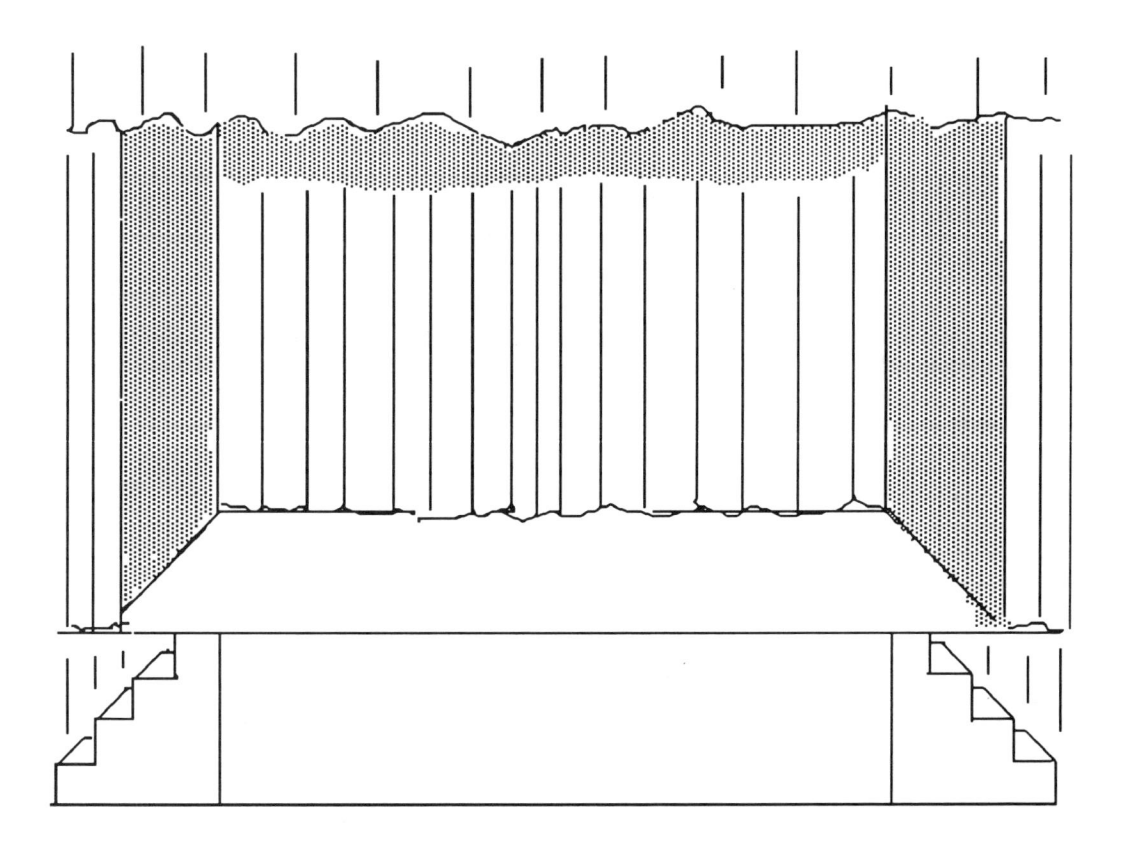

82 Personal Workbook

B. Imagine further implications of both of these conceptions of *stage* as related to counseling.

_____
_____
_____
_____
_____
_____
_____
_____
_____
_____

C. What might happen to the process of counseling if it is contained *too tightly*? Your textbook describes counseling as a "process" implying "a progressive movement toward an ultimate conclusion" (p. 36). It could be further implied that from its onset to termination there are particular tasks along the way to be addressed by both counselor and counselee before moving on to the next stage.

_____
_____
_____
_____
_____
_____
_____
_____
_____

D. **Stage Models and Their Developmental Tasks.** Freud was the first stage theorist. He set forth a conception of personality development beginning with the first year of human life and proceeding into early adulthood. The schema consists of four distinct stages and one less well-defined pre-adolescent phase. These are known as "the psychosexual stages."

PSYCHOSEXUAL STAGE	DEVELOPMENTAL TASK
oral stage	trust
anal stage	withholding and issuing power
phallic stage	interfacing the environment
latency stage	education by the elders
genital stage	self-definition and leaving home

Others have expanded Freud's developmental schema to amplify its social implications. One such author is Erikson (1980). These are known as "the psychosocial stages."

ERIKSON'S EIGHT AGES	DEVELOPMENTAL TASKS
Trust versus mistrust	To get and give in return
Autonomy versus shame and doubt	To hold on and to let go
Initiative versus guilt	To *make-like*; i.e., play
Industry versus inferiority	To make things; to make things together
Identity versus identity diffusion	To be oneself
Intimacy versus isolation	To relate self to another
Generativity versus self-absorption	To produce and care for
Ego integrity versus despair	To face not being

Another way to conceptualize the life-cycle is shown below in which each task is shown with regard to the particular function that allows it proceed.

BIRTH

	A FUNCTION OF:
Trust	safety
Negotiation	power of self in the face of limitations
Self-Direction	power of self in the environment
Application	risk-taking
Individuation	separation from primary care-givers

DEATH

Personal Workbook

Give some thought to your own place in the life cycle, and the stages through which you have passed. Consider these issues in relation to a counseling career.

E. **Travel and Odyssey.** It is critical to note that while these and virtually all suggested developmental schemas are *chronological-time-related*, they are not *chronological-time-restricted*. Freud and others have stated (often with limited success) that any stage progression is not meant to indicate a clean, linear progression, but rather a more or less meandering back and forth from onset to conclusion.

Think of it this way. How does travel differ from odyssey? *Travel* can be seen as moving from Point A to Point B in the shortest line possible. It emphasizes efficiency, economy, and reaching the destination. (See Kerényi, 1987)

- *Travel is linear.*
- *Travel stresses destination.*
- *Travel is product-focused.*

Example of travel:

SEATTLE ☞ NEW YORK CITY
fewest miles possible.

A Personal Travel Experience:

_____
_____
_____
_____
_____
_____
_____
_____
_____
_____
_____
_____
_____
_____
_____

Odyssey on the other hand can be seen as meaningful meandering, from port to port, each one indicating the next direction (it is critical to consider that odyssey is as purposeful as travel, just in a different way). It emphasizes depth of experience and the optimal integration of the richness of all that lies between the point of embarkation and the destination.

- *Odyssey is non-linear*
- *Odyssey stresses experience along the way.*
- *Odyssey is process-focused.*

For, unlike the Roman highways which cut unmercifully straight through the countryside, they run snakelike, shaped like irrationally waved lines, conforming to the contours of the land, winding, yet leading everywhere.
Kerényi, 1987, p.14

In Homer's *Odyssey*, it was necessary for Odysseus to take many side trips, and perform many arduous tasks, even descending into the Halls of Hades, before he was able to return home. The value of his odyssey lay in the ways he was tested, and in the lessons he learned along the way.

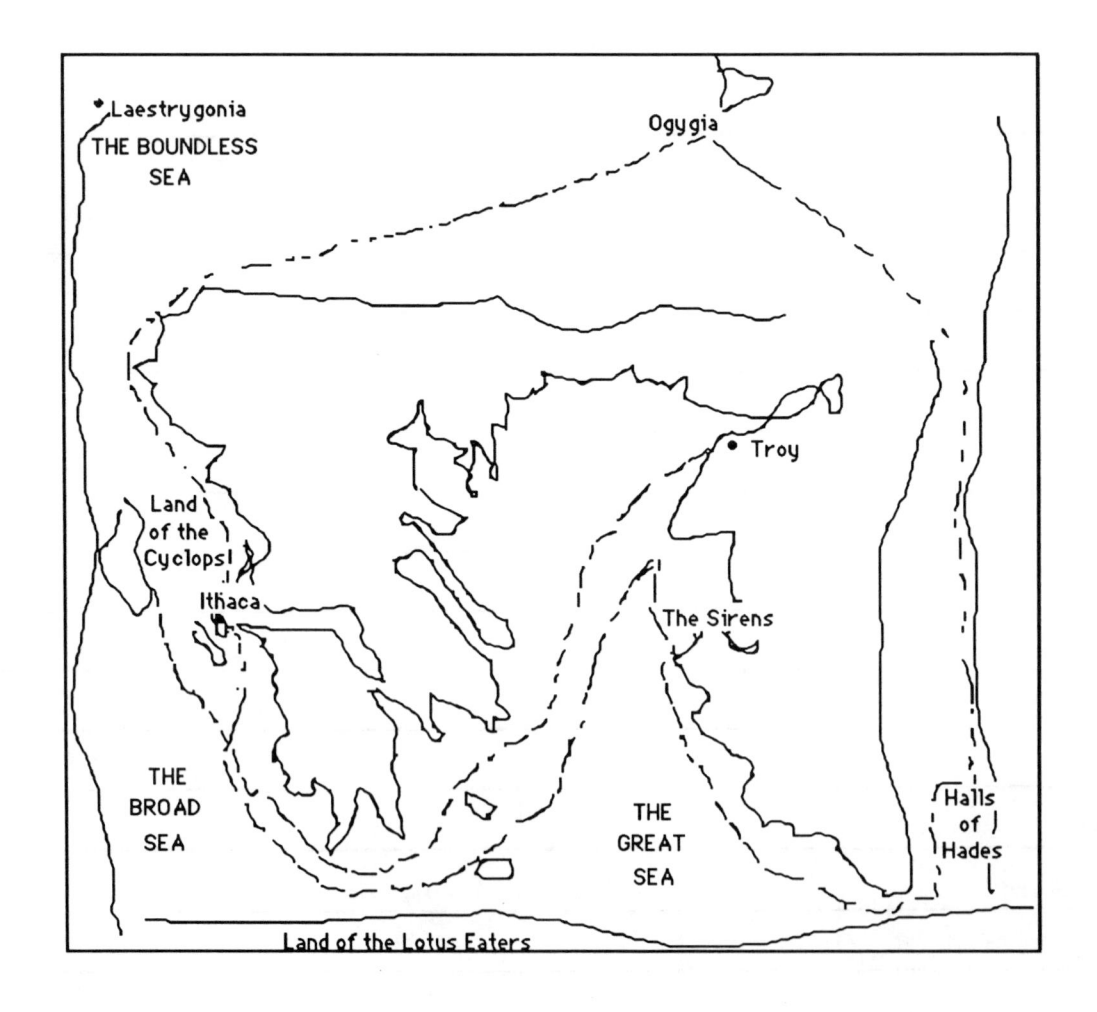

A Personal Odyssey:

88 Personal Workbook

1. Consider experiences of your own in which you have traveled and others where you have experienced odyssey. Which appeals to you most? What are the benefits and possible pit-falls of each? For example, what almost happened to Odysseus and his band by staying *too long* in the land of the lotus-eaters? With regard to your counselor education, general life experience, and relationship endeavors, how do you see the notions of travel and odyssey being applicable?

   _____
   _____
   _____
   _____

2. Now think about how the foregoing and other conceptions of personality development and archetypal life experience might be seen as metaphors for the counseling process. Counseling is about life, and moreover, it is a living phenomenon. Perhaps it is no coincidence that it can be seen as approximating the life-cycle. Your textbook sets forth five stages of counseling. What are they?

   1. _____
   2. _____
   3. _____
   4. _____
   5. _____

   What might be the developmental task(s) of each?

   1. _____
   2. _____
   3. _____
   4. _____
   5. _____

   How are the developmental victories of each stage of the counseling process carried forward to the next stage?

   _____
   _____
   _____
   _____

For further amplification of the resemblances of the process of counseling to the process of larger life-cycle development, see Harris (1986) and Garcia (1995).

The stages of the counseling process, set forth in your textbook, and the possible developmental tasks of each:

STAGES OF COUNSELING	POSSIBLE DEVELOPMENTAL TASKS
Rapport and relationship building	attachment and trust building
Assessing client problems	mutual understanding of counseling focus
Goal setting	shared responsibility; "making like".
Initiating interventions	action interface; "making things"
Termination and follow-up	self-definition and separation

How might the notions of travel and odyssey be applied to the stage conception of the counseling process as set forth by Hackney and Cormier in your textbook? Discuss with your professor and colleagues the following:

1. What about counselor flexibility with regard to respecting the client's unique process?

2. Is conclusion found in a linear direction from onset? How might onset and conclusion be different views of the same thing?

3. How does *progress* relate to and perhaps challenge the notion of *process*?

4. How might lingering too long in any stage deter clients from reaching "'home"?

5. What if the counselor is attempting to travel and the client is making an odyssey? Conversely, what if the counselor is encouraging odyssey and the client wants to travel?

F. **By The Way, What Are Skills?** According to *The Oxford English Dictionary*, the word *skill* comes from Old Norse *skil* which means "distinction, difference". It defines the term as "practical knowledge in combination with ability; cleverness, expertness. Also, an ability to perform a function, acquired or learnt with practice" (v. 15, p. 603). There are numerous skills (distinctions) you must attempt to acquire in order to become a professional counselor. Consider the following and identify possible challenges to your acquisition of each:

SKILLS	PERSONAL CHALLENGES
the skill of attending	
the skill of listening	
the skill of paraphrasing	
the skill of reflecting	
the skill of perspective-taking	
the skill of empathy	
the skill of immediacy	
the skill of assessing	
the skill of goal-setting	
the skill of intervening	
the skill of terminating	
the skill of self-care	
the skill of _____	
the skill of _____	
the skill of _____	

RAPPORT AND RELATIONSHIP

CHAPTER THREE

Hackney & Cormier

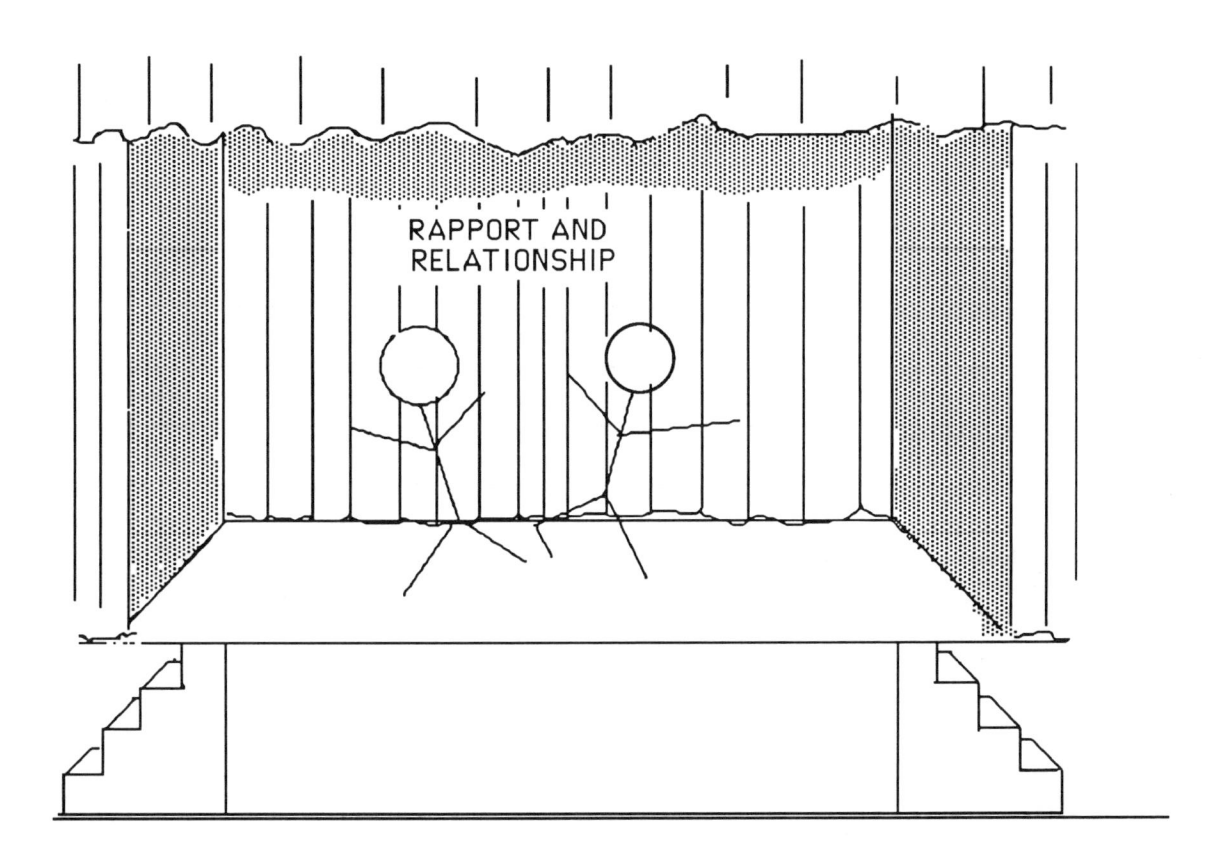

Personal Workbook

1. What do you look for, first and foremost, in a relationship?

   _____
   _____
   _____
   _____
   _____
   _____
   _____
   _____
   _____
   _____
   _____

2. From what you have learned so far about the differences in a social and professional (helping) relationship, and about yourself, what do you see that might enhance/impair your ability to establish effective professional (helping) relationships?

   _____
   _____
   _____
   _____
   _____
   _____
   _____
   _____
   _____
   _____
   _____

3. What does it mean from a social and professional perspective to:

                        SOCIAL   PROFESSIONAL

care for someone: _____   _____

attend to someone: _____   _____

understand someone: _____   _____

work with someone: _____   _____

be with someone _____   _____

4. Elaborate on what the impact to you might be from participating in a relationship in which you are not the one having your needs met beyond being paid a fee?

_____

_____

_____

_____

_____

Rogers (1957) set forth "necessary and sufficient conditions" for therapeutic change (pp. 2-3). While others have argued that these conditions may not be entirely sufficient in all clinical cases, most agree that they are necessary for the establishment and maintenance of any helping relationship regardless of the treatment modality (i.e., technique) being engaged. Rogers' conditions are:

- *Two persons are in psychological contact.*

- *The first, whom we shall term the client, is in a state of incongruence, being vulnerable or anxious.*

- *The second person, whom we shall term the therapist, is congruent or integrated in the relationship.*

- *The therapist experiences unconditional positive regard for the client.*

- *The therapist experiences an empathic understanding of the client's internal frame of reference and endeavors to communicate this experience to the client.*

- *The communication to the client of the therapist's empathic understanding and unconditional positive regard is to a minimal degree achieved.*

As you go through the following exercises, refer back to Rogers' "conditions."

5. **Establishing Psychological Contact and Communicating Rapport.**

Pair with one of your colleagues and sit facing each other directly. Select another person to be the time-keeper and to observe each of you in the role of speaker and listener. Look squarely into each other's eyes, allow a *psychological contact* to be established between the two of you in the relationship.

As you do this, you may notice the need to smile or giggle. Where does this affect come from and what might it be saying? Could the affect be anxiety? Anxiety is defined as "fear of loss in the future." What is it that one might be afraid of losing in this (or any) relationship?

When the time-keeper says "go" one of you will begin speaking. Just say whatever comes to mind for three (3) minutes. The listener just "listens;" not responding with words. At the end of the time, reverse the roles and repeat the exercise.

A. Discuss your experience as both speaker and listener. What did you discover about yourself in each role?

_____
_____
_____
_____
_____

B. How did you build rapport with the speaker without responding with words? How was that rapport communicated to the other?

_____
_____
_____
_____
_____

C. What did you find yourself saying to the other person? How safe did you feel with the listener?

_____
_____
_____
_____
_____

D. Allow the time-keeper to give each of you feedback on what she or he observed.

_____
_____
_____
_____
_____

E. Which was most comfortable for you, speaking or listening? What might account for the difference?

_____
_____
_____

6. **The Foundation of A Relationship**

   Inflate a large balloon and tie off the end. Now, select a partner and stand side-by-side; shoulder-to-shoulder. Place the inflated balloon between you at the upper arm. Imagine the balloon as both a *point of contact* that connects the two of you AS WELL AS a *boundary* that separates the two of you.

   Now, at the same time, begin pushing with your bodies toward the balloon. Note your experience as the pressure builds on the contact point/boundary. What kinds of feelings do you notice coming up?

   Now, one person begins moving away. Feel the pressure come off the contact point/boundary. Continue moving away until the balloon falls to the floor.

   Pick up the balloon and replace it between your shoulders. Again, begin pushing together toward the center until the balloon explodes.

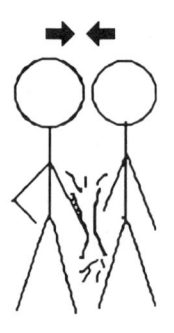

E. Now, discuss the implications of this metaphor with regard to what happens in any relationship when:

   - *the individuals in the relationship crowd the contact point/boundary (i.e., become too close)*

   - *one of the individuals does not attend to personal responsibility in maintaining the relationship*

   - *the importance of being aware at all times of just what it is that connects and separates the participants in any relationship*

   _____

   _____

   _____

   _____

   _____

   _____

7. **Congruence versus Incongruence**.

>Pick a partner with one assuming the role of "client" and the other the role of "counselor." The client reads the following statements, smiling and laughing as the statements are being read. "Well, last night I had a huge fight with my mother. She is such a bitch. You know, sometimes I just hate her and last night I really felt like I wanted to kill her. She screamed at me, slapped me, and left me crying.
>
>The counselor now paraphrases what the client stated communicating affect more closely associated with the painful material communicated by the content (i.e., pleasure and mirth are not congruent with violent, angry behavior). At the same time the therapist attempts to acknowledge the client's difficulty (i.e., incongruence) in recognizing in a genuine way the pain of the story.

A. Now, discuss together the felt experience of incongruence and congruence. What might the counselor's congruence in the moment communicate to the client?

_____
_____
_____
_____
_____
_____
_____

B. In the role of counselor, what do you learn about yourself with regard to the awesome task of becoming congruent and integrated in the helping relationship?

_____
_____
_____
_____
_____
_____
_____

8. Empathy versus Identification.

> Procure two ordinary household clothespins. Pick a partner and sit facing each other. One person attaches a clothespin to her or his chin so that it is pinching, yet not injuring the face. The other person attempts to take the perspective of the one in pain.

Rogers (1957) suggested that empathy necessarily involves an "as if" perspective (i.e., it is "as if" I am in your place, yet I am not in a literal sense). The one without the clothespin on her or his face now attempts to experience something like what the other is experiencing. Empathy is not only to be experienced by the therapist, but also must be communicated to the client in order for therapeutic movement to occur (Rogers, 1957). Therefore, the one relating empathically to the one in pain now lets the other know in some way the felt empathy. How does this happen? With words, body posture, eye movements, etc.

> Now, the one attempting to be empathic places a clothespin on his or her own face in exactly the same place as the other.

Can this person now say that she or he *knows* how the other feels? In other words, what does it feel like to identify with the other given two similar situations? How might this kind of identification thwart the helper's ability to be empathic? Remove the clothespins and discuss:

A. How might identification lead to building rapport, yet impede counselor empathy?

_____
_____
_____

B. If both client and counselor are experiencing (or have experienced) similar pain, how might the counselor be led to feel his or her own pain versus that of the client? set aside her or his own pain and move into a place of empathy?

_____
_____
_____

C. *Reflect on your personal capacity not only to experience empathy, but also to communicate it.*

_____
_____
_____

9. **Social Life versus Professional Life**. Consider how your daily experiences might work consistently to encourage your incongruence and identification versus congruence and empathy? Read through the following scenarios:

> You are feeling sad having had a fight with your best friend. You meet a co-worker in the hallway and she says:
>
> *"Good morning, how are you?"* (smiling)
>
> *"Fine, thanks, and you?"* (smiling, even though you feel anything but fine inside)

What feelings might you actually be experiencing inside?

___

What would keep you from expressing authentically your feelings in this social situation? Consider:

- *lack of safety (i.e., trust)*
- *the socio-cultural maxim of "smile and the world smiles with you; cry and you cry alone"*
- *absence of genuiness on the part of the person inquiring as to "how you are doing"*

___

What are other ways the general social milieu encourages inauthentic expression of feelings?

___

You are driving along and pass the scene of an car accident. Emergency workers are treating an injured person. Your mind flashes back to an accident in which you were injured a year ago. You feel intense feelings for the person you now see lying on the street. What might some of those feelings be? Consider:

- *sadness*

- *fear*

- *compassion*

How might your past experience cause you to *identify* with the injured person thus promoting feelings of *sympathy* instead of *empathy*? Who might these feelings really be for?

_____

_____

_____

_____

You read an account in the newspaper of an individual arrested for brutally murdering a child. What kind of feelings do you have toward this perpetrator? Are you able to experience positive regard for the individual who committed this crime? Contrast the feelings you would have immediately for the child with those you experience toward the perpetrator. Can you see them both as victims? How might society reinforce one's feelings of anger and blame toward an individual who would commit a crime such as this?

_____

_____

_____

_____

What would you have to recognize and resolve with regard to your personal feelings if you were called upon to work in a counseling relationship with the person who did this to a child?

_____

_____

_____

_____

Discuss with your professor and colleagues how positive regard may be easy enough to talk about, yet much more of a task in terms of experiencing.

_____

_____

_____

Observe over the course of a week, how many times, in social encounters, you communicate feelings to another by way of your words and facial gestures, etc., that you are *not* experiencing inside.

Monday	Tuesday	Wednesday	Thursday	Friday	Saturday	Sunday

Summary: The stage of *rapport* and *relationship* is the foundation of the professional helping relationship. Consider the implications of the victories and failures in this stage for future stages.

___

Freud (1933), referring to his stage conception of instinctual development, wrote:

> Our attitude to the phases of the organization of the libido has in general shifted a little. Whereas earlier we chiefly emphasized the way in which each of them passed away before the next, our attention now is directed to the facts that show us how much of each earlier phase persists alongside of and behind the later configurations and obtains a permanent representation in the libidinal economy and character of the subject. (p. 100)

Consider the implications of Freud's comments on the psychosexual stage development model to the stage development model of helping presented in your textbook. From the victories realized in the stage of *relationship* and *rapport*, what might "persist alongside of and behind" the next stage of counseling?

___

ASSESSING CLIENT PROBLEMS
CHAPTER FOUR
Hackney & Cormier

*True education can only start from naked reality,
not from a delusive ideal.*
C.G. Jung

Re-read Chapter 4 of your textbook. The authors recognize the reality that "defining a 'problem' is a very difficult process" (p. 115). Notice that the authors use the word *process* here which means that assessing client problems is itself more than a one-time effort. This activity *takes on a life of its own*, as do all elements of counseling.

1. What are the essential questions that, according to your textbook, underlie the clinical assessment process?

2. What is the "inherent trap" identified by your textbook that counselors face in the assessment process?

3. How will you as a professional counselor communicate to your clients that you accept and are seeking to understand their presenting problems and at the same time avoid the temptation of problem-solving and thus perhaps too closely identify the person of the client with a problem and rob them of deeper personal understanding and empowerment?

104 Personal Workbook

4. The helping professions have been influenced by numerous paradigms of "helping and coping." (Brickman, et al, 1982). Of these perhaps the most influential has been the "medical model." This paradigm invests authority in *experts*. At this very moment you are working toward recognition as an expert: educated, trained, and certified to provide professional counseling to those who seek it. In addition to its emphasis on expertise, the medical model tends to be reactionary. It examines, diagnoses, and then prescribes treatment for a particular problem as manifested in the ailing organism. The medical model relies on empirical research to create an arsenal of treatments (e.g., medications) to eliminate disease and suffering. Think about the apparent resemblance between medicine and professional counseling. Identify other influences of the medical model on professional counseling.

MEDICINE	COUNSELING
physician (expert)	professional counselor (expert)
symptom	problem
examination	assessment
diagnosis	strategy
treatment	intervention
discharge	termination
recovery	outcome

_____

_____

_____

5. Let us consider further the correlation between the medical image of *symptom* and the counseling image of *problem*.

According to Shipley (1945), the term *symptom* comes from the Greek *symptoma*, meaning "mischance" which originates from *sympiplein*, meaning "to fall together, to happen to." *Taber's Cyclopedic Medical Dictionary* defines symptom as "any perceptible change in the body or its functions that indicates disease or the kind of phases of disease" (p. 1798). Implicit in the understanding of this definition is that the symptom indicates something that is to be *corrected or perhaps eliminated in order for the organism to resume a healthy state.* Consider the contradictions of this notion with regard to counseling. According to your textbook how does one determine if counseling has been successful? List those criteria below:

_____

_____

_____

_____

Notice that the textbook says nothing about *eliminating* the problem or *problem-solving*. Rather the description seems far more to indicate that a successful client experience in counseling will result in a *better understanding of the problem,* or perhaps *new and different approaches to the integration of the problem toward more optimal client functioning.* Still, how prevalent is the notion that counseling involves the identification of some dysfunction and its elimination? Think about how insurance carriers, as conditions for payment for counseling services, may insist on diagnosis, treatment, and indication of symptom relief (i.e., behavioral change).

6. Search through the commercial ads in popular magazines such as those that might be found in the waiting rooms of physicians and dentists. *How many ads do you find for pain relievers and other agents intended to provide symptom relief?* How many ads do you find offering agents that encourage further discovery that might involve even more pain than the presenting problem? How often do you find these words in the ads?

faster	now, even faster relief
even more effective than . . .	total relief
now with "super ingredient x"	nothing offers speedier relief
improved pain relief formula	won't upset your stomach
speed stains away	high performance formula
whiter, even faster	brighter, fresher breath
kills germs immediately	easier to take than ever

How might this kind of constant consumer instruction via the popular media affect the expectations clients bring to counseling?

_____
_____
_____
_____
_____
_____
_____
_____
_____
_____
_____
_____

106　Personal Workbook

7. Does professional counseling practice what it preaches when it comes to assessing client problems? Refer back to Remley's (1992) statements of that which distinguishes counseling from other helping professions (p.48). What are those criteria?

_____

_____

_____

Still, in practical application, how much does counseling remain problem-focused? Discuss this with your professor and colleagues. Identify ways you, as a member of the counseling profession, might contribute to furthering the identity of the counseling profession toward:

- *pro-activity versus re-activity*
- *holism versus reductionism*
- *awareness versus diagnosis*
- *empowerment versus treatment*
- *wellness-driven versus disease-driven*

_____

_____

_____

_____

_____

_____

_____

_____

_____

_____

_____

_____

Part 3 Stages and Skills of Counseling **107**

8. Discuss the following ideas with counseling practitioners:

A. How many clients come in *without* some problem, simply to explore and find ways to live more optimally? How might this be related to the ways in which mental health care has been identified by consumers with medical care? In other words, how often do clients believe that they must have a *problem* in order to seek counseling?

B. How many clients are seeking symptom relief as opposed to more complex ways of functioning in the world? How might this be related to human nature with regard to the "pleasure-principle?"

C. A mainstream culture that is *product-focused* may discourage the stated *process-focus* of professional counseling. How might this explain the reasons that members of cultures outside mainstream are less likely to seek professional counseling?

D. The current state of health care insurance may influence the counseling practitioner to remain symptom-focused. How can counselors address this and other practical realities of practice and at the same time deal with the incongruence this might present with regard to *who we say we are and what we actually do*? How does one balance communication to the client that presenting problems are accepted and material for deeper understanding without taking the action of "rescuer" and robbing clients of critical developmental opportunities?

108   Personal Workbook

9. One writer who has suggested some ideas that could assist counseling in furthering its own unique approach to assessing client problems is the Swiss psychiatrist Carl Jung (1950, CW). (Note: the brackets are used to amend the language of the writer that could be heard as sexist). He wrote:

> ... a [person] drives a nail into the wall and we ask ... why [he or she] is doing it; if [he/she] answers that it is to hang [his/her] coat there, then [the behavior] is purposive because it makes sense. But if [he/she] answers it is because [he/she] happened to hold a hammer and nail in [his/her] hands, [the behavior] is a symptom, or at least [he/she] wants it to appear as such. (Vol. 18, ¶ 1309)

From Jung's thinking we might begin to see client problems as *purposive* and *functional*. Therefore, rather than something to be eliminated, the problem (i.e., symptom) becomes a phenomenon to be amplified, explored, and followed to its purposeful origin.

With this in mind, go back and re-read the Sufi story on page 40 of this book.

10. Now, consider ways you might create a congruent and culturally competent definition of the term *problem*. Here are some ideas:

something to be identified	vs	invitation to be followed to its purposeful depth
a single defining characteristic	vs	only one dimension of the client
a hindrance to effective living	vs	a developmental opportunity
a diagnosis	vs	a question
a troublesome situation to be eliminated	vs	something to be understood

What ideas do you come up with?

_____
_____
_____
_____
_____
_____
_____
_____
_____
_____

11. **Intake or History Interviews.** How do you define the term *inter*-view? Do you see it as a one-sided enterprise in which one person is attempting to understand the other or do you see it in its more literal interpretation as "a view BETWEEN two people?"

    A.   As the professional counselor goes through the intake process as set forth in your textbook, what kinds of conclusions might the client be drawing? For example, what might the client construe about the counselor from a particular question the counselor asks, or the manner in which it is asked? Does the counselor take written notes during the interview. What are the areas of focus the counselor presents (e.g., past history, current level of functioning; feelings, thoughts, behaviors, relationships)?

_____

_____

_____

_____

    B.   Identify your own possible professional insecurities that might cause you to be listening too carefully for a "problem" to be solved.

_____

_____

_____

_____

    C.   What might lead the counselor to be "looking for something with a needle that could be found with a broom?" For example, the client who is complaining of feeling "nervous and jittery." The client reveals that she or he daily drinks fifteen cups of coffee and eats ten chocolate bars. The counselor overlooks this organic reality in search of some psychological etiology for the problem.

_____

_____

_____

_____

110 Personal Workbook

12. **The Intake Interview.** Reprinted below is the outline of the intake interview from your textbook. Answer the questions and give the information required in Sections I - V "as if" you were the client embarking on the experience of professional counseling. Refer to the text for detailed questions in each section.

The Intake Interview

I. *Identifying data.*

   A. Client's name, address, and telephone number at which the client can be reached.

   B. Age, sex, marital status, occupation (or school class and year).

II. *Presenting problems, both primary and secondary.*

   A. How much doe the problem interfere with the client's everyday functioning?

   B. How does the problem manifest itself? What are the thoughts, feelings, etc., that are associated with it? What observable behavior is associated with it?

   C. How often does the problem arise? How long has the problem existed? When did it first appear?

   D. Can the client identify a pattern of events that surround the problem? When does it occur? With whom? What happens before and following its occurrence? Can the client anticipate the onset of the problem?

   E. What caused the client to decide to enter counseling at this time?

III. *Client's current life setting.*

   A. How does the client spend a typical day or week?

   B. What social and religious activities, recreational activities, etc. are present?

   C. What is the nature of the client's vocational and/or educational situation?

   D. What special characteristics about the client, cultural, ethnic, religious, lifestyle, age, and physical or other challenges must the client address in an ongoing manner?

IV. *Family history.*

   A. Father's and mother's ages, occupations, descriptions of their personalities, family roles, relationships of each to the other and each to the client and other siblings.

   B. Names and ages of brothers and sisters; their present life situations; relationship between client and siblings.

   C. Is there any history of mental illness in the family?

   D. Descriptions of family stability, including number of jobs held, number of family moves (and reasons), etc.

V.   *Personal history.*

   A.   Medical history.

   B.   Educational history.

   C.   Military service history.

   D.   Vocational history.

   E.   Sexual and marital history.

VI. *Description of the client during the interview.*

VII. *Summary and recommendations.*

Now, respond honestly to these questions:

A. What would you want the counselor to construe from these data you have provided?

___

B. What would you want the counselor to see as the "problem?"

___

C. What might the counselor mistake as the "problem" thus censoring a deeper lying message?

Personal Workbook

D. What might you see as the functional aspect of your statement of problem?

_____
_____
_____
_____
_____
_____
_____

E. Go back to the part of this book where you talked about your cultural heritage. How might this impact that which you would readily "disclose" during an intake interview?

_____
_____
_____
_____
_____
_____
_____
_____

F. How would rapport and relationship (or lack thereof) with the counselor influence your responses to the items of the intake interview?

_____
_____
_____
_____
_____
_____
_____
_____

G. Complete Section VI. of the Intake Interview - acting now as the "counselor" responding to what you as "client" provided on the intake interview.

114 Personal Workbook

13. As your textbook states, the counselor is called upon to gather accurate information, and make educated guesses without "elaborate inferences." It is important to reiterate the caveat that any guesses not be made prematurely. Consider the situation of the individual mentioned on page 117 of the textbook. It indicates a male client who reports that he is self-conscious around women. Let's call him Eric.

   A. The counselor accepts this report as Eric's "presenting problem." What does Eric want to change?

   B. How might the gender of the counselor impact the result of Eric's dialogue about the problem?

   C. How might Eric's situation reflect a coping strategy that has protected him from his possible fear of intimacy?

   D. How might Eric's experience with women indicate an adaptive response to protect him from his latent authentic sexual orientation?

   E. How can the counselor remain open to possibilities of further dimensions to Eric's problem without engaging in reckless interpretations and miss the obvious?

14. **Clarification of Language in Assessing Client Problems.** Often clients use popular or sweeping language in talking about their problems.

A. Consider the following and attribute the various meanings you associate with each:

weird	fuzzy	bizarre	icky	crud
sucks	shitty	blahs	bummin'	totally bummed
bummed out	losing it	dickhead	loser	bitch
bastard	freaking	freaked out	killer	queer
duh	buzzed	buzzin'	really . . .	like . . .
wrecked	prick	pissed	really pissed	totally pissed
geek	trippin'	totally gorgeous	lost ball in high weeds	awesome
hate	fucked up	love	kill	wreck
no way	way	life (as in *get a...*)	blitzed	blasted
blown apart	ripped	stressed	totally stressed	down
wasted	flaky	hairball	alien	mess (as in "I'm a . . . ")
lame	funk	slug	vege	tight

_____

_____

_____

_____

_____

B. Consider how the enterprise of assessing client problems in an efficacious manner is further complicated when the counselor is working across cultures differing from their own. Identify as many terms as you can that might come from clients of diverse populations and could confuse the counselor in client problem assessment. Here are some examples. Do you know what they mean?

the man	top/bottom	butch/fem	mariposa
mestiza	whore	queen	camp
saudade	sapatão	oreo	word

_____

_____

_____

_____

_____

_____

116 Personal Workbook

C. Pick a partner and role play the following counselor/client scenario. Suppose that the client has completed the intake report and the counselor is now asking for some elaboration.

> Counselor: So, Melody, I have some information from you now. Tell me more about what brings you to counseling.
>
> Client: Well, it's like . . . you know . . . it's like, I'm so totally stressed right now. My classes are so lame and all my professors are such hairballs. And, I'm like not sleeping. But, it's like . . . it's like . . . it's like the real bummer is my boyfriend, Todd. He is like so totally gorgeous; I mean like, WHOA . . . drop dead gorgeous and I'm so like totally warped over him. But lately he's been seeing some other people . . . like we agreed we'd both do. But, you know, it's like really weirdin' me out. You know? There's this one slut he's seein' named Monica and I'm thinkin' in my head they're like totally poking, but deep down I feel like Todd really loves me, so maybe they're not So, I don't know. And I'm kinda dating Rick, but he's like a total loser. Do you know what I'm saying?

Now, the counselor responds to the client toward better understanding of this brief sketch of the problem Melody is presenting. Perhaps the counselor might use the immediately functional question:

Melody, help me to understand what you mean by _____.

How many times can you use this question without communicating to the client that you are completely out of touch? From the client's statements above, select the problem descriptors you would choose to ask to be further clarified. What seems most important about these? Are the terms you chose to pay attention to

- feelings
- thoughts
- behaviors
- relationships

_____
_____
_____
_____

What might this tell you about that which you hear *first* in client problem assessment? Are these the aspects to which you pay attention in assessing and dealing with your own problems?

_____
_____
_____
_____

Part 3   Stages and Skills of Counseling   **117**

Continue the role play to the point where you feel you have a reasonably clear understanding of Melody's problem. What is it? How do you check it out with her? Practice using both open-ended and closed-ended questions in your assessment. What does she want to do with you in counseling relative to this problem? In your own fantasy what would you like for her to do with the problem? How would you keep this fantasy out of the counseling milieu with Melody?

_____

_____

_____

_____

_____

_____

_____

_____

_____

_____

_____

_____

_____

_____

_____

_____

15. Often written instruments (i.e., paper and pencil tests) are used by counselors in assessing client's problems. Consult *Mental Measurements Yearbook* for further description and elaboration of these instruments. Also, refer to the ACA Code of Ethics (Appendix A of your textbook) section on *tests and measurements* for critical ethical concerns in administering and drawing conclusions from these instruments.

DEVELOPING COUNSELING GOALS

CHAPTER FIVE

Hackney & Cormier

*It is good to have an end to journey towards,
but it is the journey that matters in the end.*
Ursula K. LeGuin

Reread Chapter 5 of your textbook.

1. According to *The Oxford English Dictionary*, the etymology of the term *goal* suggests derivation from an Old English *gál*, meaning *obstacle, barrier*, apparently derived from *gaelan*, meaning *to hinder, delay*.

    Your textbook argues strongly in favor of the activity of goal-setting as part of the counseling process. What are some of the arguments offered?

    _____
    _____
    _____
    _____
    _____
    _____

    Here, as in all aspects of counseling, there are exceptions. For example, while a goal may provide a boundary and something to work toward, some clients might find the goal limiting, or even a hindrance to their own unique process. Consider the case of a client who wants to be an actor and sets that realization as a outcome goal for counseling. Along the way however, it becomes more and more obvious to the client that he or she has no talent for acting, yet shows considerable promise as a writer. However, because the goal to be an actor is so firmly established, the client is unable (unwilling) to yield in order to optimize his/her unique potentials and limitations.

    Compare goal to direction:

Goal is specific.	Direction is less specific.
Goal is unidirectional.	Direction is multi-directional.
Goal provides focus.	Direction provides areas of focus.
Goal is travel-oriented.	Direction is odyssey-oriented.

    How might clients who are more tolerant of ambiguity find goals limiting? Give an example of such a client. How might clients who need structure and cannot work with ambiguity find direction too open-ended and contribute to a feeling that nothing is happening in counseling? Give an example of such a client. How could you see goals perhaps working more effectively in *short-term* counseling and direction more likely to be called for in *long-term* counseling? How would the temperament and typology of the counselor influence either the use of goals or directions?

    _____
    _____
    _____
    _____
    _____

Personal Workbook

What does your textbook offer as three (3) functions of goals?

_____

_____

_____

_____

3. Take a look at your own experience with goals/directions. First, recall a goal you set for yourself which you attained. What were the conditions that contributed to its becoming realized?

_____

_____

_____

_____

Now, recall a goal you set for yourself which you did not attain. What were the conditions that contributed to its not becoming realized?

_____

_____

_____

_____

Recall a direction you set for yourself that led you to unexpected success. What were the conditions that contributed to this happening?

_____

_____

_____

_____

Recall a direction you set for yourself that wound up with you becoming more and more confused. What were the conditions that contributed to this?

_____

_____

_____

_____

Given you worldview, temperament, and general developmental level, which do you prefer for yourself most often - goals or directions?

4. Goal implies action (after all., the first two letters of the word spell *go*!). How might goals motivate clients to increase their active participation in the counseling process? How might an action-oriented counselor become over zealous about the client's goal-setting and frustrated if the client offers meaningful resistance to the attainment of the goal? How might goal-setting be more of a challenge for the counselor who is not goal-oriented and is instead more direction oriented? How could you see goals and goal-setting being of more appeal to counselors with a behavioral or cognitive orientation than perhaps with those of more affective or inter-personal orientations? How could you see a task-oriented counselor unwittingly punishing a client for not reaching established goals or unwittingly over-rewarding a client for reaching established goals?

5. What might happen if the counselor becomes overly-attached to process goals and is unable to allow for the client's unique process in moving through the counseling experience?

What might happen if the client becomes overly-attached to outcome goals and fails?

Part 3   Stages and Skills of Counseling **123**

6. **Different Strokes for Different Folks**. Compare the ways *goals* might be indicated for particular populations and *directions* be indicated for others:

    Examples:

    child or adolescent
    high degree of impulsivity
    low tolerance for ambiguity
    need for "exsight" via concrete developmental markers

    middle-aged adult
    post-conformist level of ego development
    high tolerance for ambiguity
    high ability for insight

    For further elaboration of these conceptions, see Loevinger (1976).

7. **Elements of Positive Outcome Goals**. What does your textbook suggest as three (3) elements of positive outcome goals?

    _____

    _____

    _____

    _____

    _____

8. What does the textbook suggest with regard to obstacles to developing specific goals? How might unreasonable expectations from either the client or the counselor serve to sabotage goal setting and realization?

    _____

    _____

    _____

    _____

    _____

9. **Confrontation**. What does this word mean to you in a social sense? What does the textbook say about its reputation?

    _____

    _____

    _____

    _____

    _____

124 Personal Workbook

Literally the word *confrontation* means, "facing with, as in to stand face to face." There is nothing about the term that suggests conflict although for many it has become so associated. As the textbook points out, confrontation is an essential response in counseling. It is used to point out incongruence and discrepancy that are probably not in the client's awareness. Think about how your own socialization/enculturation might make the use of confrontation uncomfortable for you?

_____

_____

_____

_____

_____

_____

10. **Work Your "Buts" Off**. The textbook gives several examples of confrontation responses. Note that the confrontation response is most often a compound sentence pairing two typically disparate thoughts. Refer to Festinger (1957) for a review of *cognitive dissonance*. In other words the clinical intention of the confrontation is to raise the client's dissonance around a particular field of experience. One of the examples used in your textbook is: "You say school isn't very satisfying, but your grades are excellent."

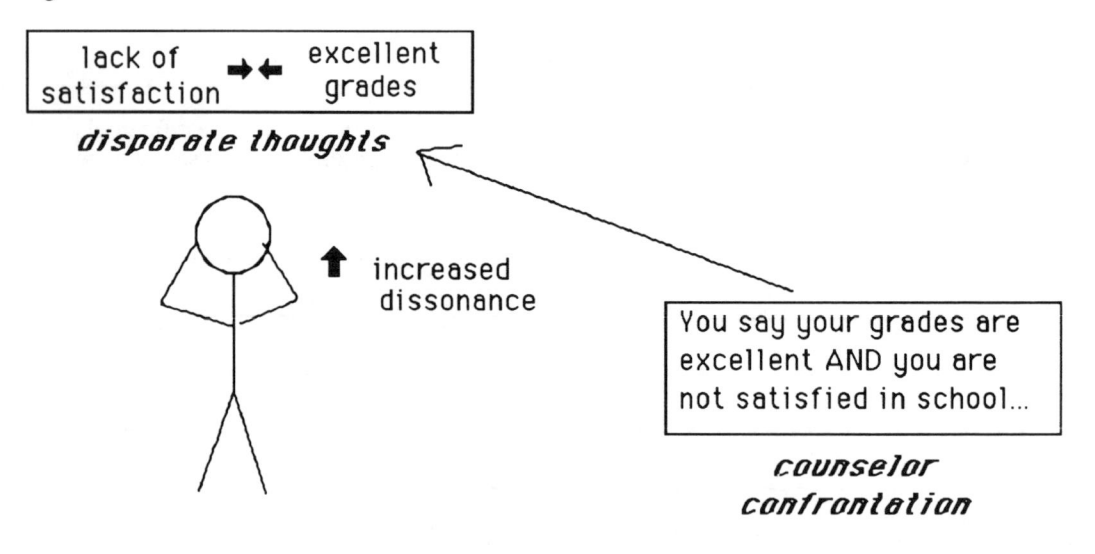

Instead of using *but* to connect the two thoughts in an effective confrontation, what about the use of *and*? *But* tends to carry much social baggage as in the famous, "I like you, BUT..... *And* tends to be more neutral than *but* and may be less likely to cause one of the thoughts of the confrontation to invalidate the other. Go back through the examples of confrontation given in the textbook and replace some of the *buts* with *ands*. What do you think?

_____

_____

_____

11. **The Ability-Potential Response.** What are the risks associated with the use of this response? Why is it as important for the counselor to assist clients in identifying *limitations* as well as *abilities*?

12. What are some of the cross-cultural issues associated with goal-setting? For example, what if the counselor is from a culture that tends to emphasize the individual (e.g., Caucasian-American) and is working in goal-setting with a client from a culture that tends to emphasize the group (e.g., Japanese-American). Give examples of clinical errors the culturally incompetent counselor might make here.

126 Personal Workbook

DEFINING STRATEGIES AND INTERVENTIONS

CHAPTER SIX

Hackney & Cormier

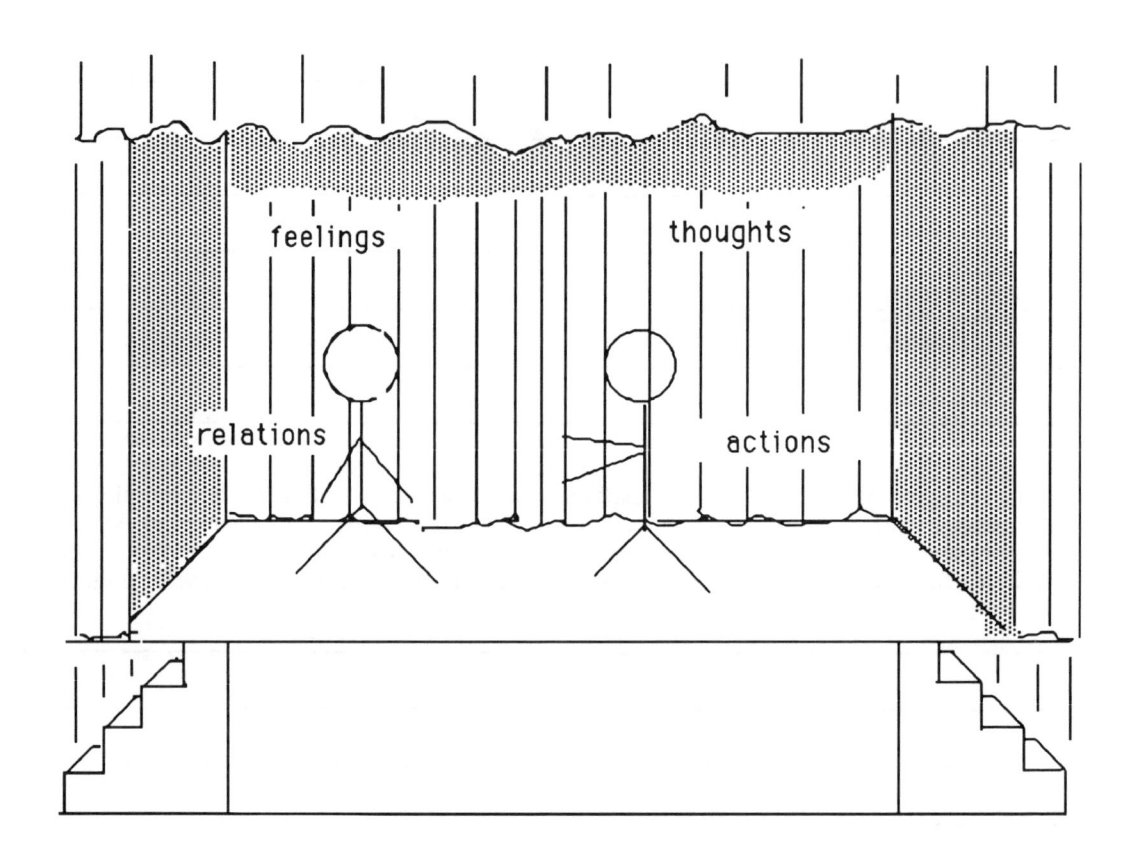

Part 3   Stages and Skills of Counseling   **127**

Reread Chapter 6 in your textbook.

1. **The Working Alliance.** Bordin (1983) has described the elements of the relationship that must exist between counselor and counselee in order for a therapeutic outcome to be possible. He called this the "therapeutic working alliance." The elements of the therapeutic working alliance are:

    - *Mutually agreed-upon goals.*
    - *Tasks.*
    - *Bonds*

    What do you understand each of these terms to mean?

A. mutually agreed-upon goals _____
    _____

B. tasks _____
    _____

C. bonds _____
    _____

2. **Difference versus Sameness.** The textbook raises the question of whether or not a culture-specific approach is the most workable in terms of establishing the therapeutic working alliance. Margolis & Rungta (1986) have addressed this question in terms of arguing that while all people are different, *it is critical for the counselor not to lose the person in the difference.* They have suggested that while it is essential that helping professionals be aware of the countless diverse ways persons make meaning of the world, it is also necessary to consider universals that all persons share as members of the human community. They argue that all persons who come into counseling are concerned with:

    Identity (self-concept)

    Self-esteem

    Validation of experience

    Empowerment

    Discuss these with your professor and colleagues. What other universals can you think of that all persons share alongside that which separates us?

    _____
    _____
    _____
    _____
    _____

4. **Your Individual Predispositions and Preferences**. Suppose you entered a room and there were four groups of people there. To which group would you most naturally be drawn?

feelers

thinkers

relaters

doers

A. What is it about you that would cause you to be most readily attracted to this group?

_____
_____
_____
_____
_____

B. How would you respond to the other groups?

_____
_____
_____
_____
_____

C. **The Myers-Briggs Type Indicator** (MBTI). One piece of information that might assist you in better understanding the manner in which you would approach defining counseling strategies and interventions is the Myers-Briggs Type Indicator. The instrument is based on Carl Jung's "psychological types" (1923) and measures the respondent's preferences for particular *ways of being in the world, taking in information from the environment, acting on that information.* The instrument utilizes an "electrical model" that shows fundamental oppositional polarities and the valences that exist between them. It includes:

→
←
ATTITUDES

extroversion--- introversion
(preference for the outer world of people and things   (preference for the inner world of ideas)

FUNCTIONS

sensing-- intuition
(preference for taking in data via the five senses)   (preference for taking in data via the sixth sense)

thinking-- feeling
(preference for making decisions via cognitions)   (preference for making decisions via affects)

LIFESTYLE ORIENTATION

judging-- perceiving
(preference for a planned, organized lifestyle)   (preference for a spontaneous lifestyle)

Schedule an appointment at your university's counseling or testing center and complete the MBTI. Be certain that you will be given feedback on the results from a counselor who understands the intended use of the MBTI and can work with it beyond a simple parlor game. For further readings, consult Jung (1923, CW, Vol. 6) or contact:

>Center for the Application of Psychological Types
>2720 N.W. 6th St.
>Gainesville, FL 32609
>904-375-0160

Once you have your results of the MBTI, consider how what you have reported as preferences on the instrument might suggest your approach to defining strategies and interventions in your clinical work. Reread the case illustration on page 198 of the textbook. Think about how your particular preferences might impact the ways you would view clients and the problems they bring to counseling. How might the *thinking/feeling* preference draw you to a particular theoretical base? How might the *judging/perceiving* preference impact the way you work to define a counseling strategy? What might the instrument tell you about less developed aspects of your personality that would warrant further development in order for you to be more systematically eclectic and flexible in your selection of strategies and interventions with diverse clients.

_____

_____

_____

130 Personal Workbook

5. **Defining a Strategy**.

   A. How do you typically approach planning and decision-making in your personal life? Do you tend to collect data about the issue, evaluate logically, and act? Do you tend to act, evaluate affectively or intuitively what happened, and then collect data to determine how well you did? Think about a recent experience in your life where you were faced with a decision. How did you handle it? Is this typical for you?

   _____

   _____

   _____

   B. **The Airplane Landing Analogy**. Strategic planning and intervention in counseling can be likened to a pilot's landing of an airplane. The first thing the pilot has do is find

   > *the state in which the airport is located* . . . . . .
   >
   > *then the county or parish in which the airport is located*
   >
   > *then the city in which the airport is located* . . . .
   >
   > *then the airport*
   >
   > *then the runway*

   In other words the pilot must consider the *widest set of possibilities* first, then gradually work toward the *narrowest set of possibilities*. The plane is equipped with sophisticated instrumentation to perform the tasks and ensure the safety of the passengers and crew. Following this analogy think about what the textbook offers on pages 199 - 205. With what are counselors equipped to perform these tasks and ensure the safety of all parties involved? How might poor strategic planning along with too early intervention lead to a "therapeutic crash?"

6. **Personalizing Your Theoretical Understandings**. James Hillman (1975) observed,

   > Each psychology is a confession, and the worth of a psychology for another lies not in the places where he [she] can identify with it because it satisfies his [her] psychic needs, but where it provokes him [her] to work out his [her] own psychology in response. (p. xii)

   Turn to page 214 in the textbook. Look over the various "psychologies" listed and described there. With which one(s) do you identify most readily/least readily? Refer back to the section of this workbook in which you talked about your socialization and cultural origin. Also, look back to the discussion of the MBTI. What does all of this tell you?

   _____

   _____

   _____

Part 3   Stages and Skills of Counseling   **131**

From the theories and therapies shown on page 214 of the textbook, choose the one you are most drawn to. What is the name of the theory/therapy? Who is the author of this theory/therapy?

_____

_____

Now, choose the one you are least drawn to. What is the name of this theory/therapy? Who is the author of this theory/therapy?

_____

_____

Read a major work of the theorist with which you *most identify* and of the theorist with which you *least identify*.

7.   **Theorists and their Confessions.**   See if you can match the following:

A.	Sigmund Freud	J.	Abraham Maslow
B.	Fritz Perls	K.	Alfred Adler
C.	B.F. Skinner	L.	Carl Jung
D.	Kurt Lewin	M.	Alexander Lowen
E.	Albert Ellis	N.	Arnold Lazarus
F.	Rollo May	O.	Carl Rogers
G.	John B. Watson	P.	Harry Stack Sullivan
H.	William James	Q.	Karen Horney
I.	Erik Erikson	R.	William Glasser

_____   1.   set out to train as a minister and switched to psychology following a trip to China

_____   2.   left academic psychology due to a divorce scandal and became an advertising executive

_____   3.   often described as a psychologist who wrote like a novelist with a novelist brother who wrote like a psychologist

_____   4.   contracted tuberculosis, spent two years in a sanitarium, and emerged to publish a major work on the nature of anxiety

_____   5.   as a child spent many hours designing contraptions, such as a device to separate ripe from unripe berries, and a steam cannon to launch potato and carrot plugs over neighboring houses

_____   6.   at fourteen received an essay entitled "The Art of Becoming An Original Writer in Three Days" which ended with the suggestion that one take a few sheets of paper and for three days write down "without any falsification or hypocrisy, everything that comes into your head"

_____   7.   medical dissertation was entitled *On the Psychology of So-Called Occult Phenomena* (1902)

_____   8.   worked at the Goldstein Institute for Brain Damaged Soldiers in Frankfurt

_____   9.   hospitalized nine times as a child mainly with nephritis

_____   10. served as consulting psychiatrist at a state facility for the treatment of delinquent adolescent girls

_____   11. engaged in weightlifting, body building, and wrestling to overcome being skinny and being the target of bullies

_____   12. a former patient of Wilhelm Reich who extended and developed Reich's "character-analytic-vegetotherapy"

132 Personal Workbook

_____ 13. at 4 years of age almost died of pneumonia and at that time made the decision to become a physician

_____ 14. at 16 recorded in a personal diary this entry: "Why is everything beautiful on earth given to me, only not the highest thing, not love! I have a heart so needing love."

_____ 15. having dropped out of two art schools to resume extensive wanderings wrote, "No doubt my best friends will insist that I needed to name this crisis and see it in everybody else in order to really come to terms with it in myself."

_____ 16. the eventual founder of a needs-based theory whose mother had many years earlier bashed the heads of two stray kittens against a wall the child had brought home, killing them

_____ 17. had a reputation for difficulty with interpersonal relationships and developed an interpersonal theory of psychiatry

_____ 18. a former foot-soldier in the German army, re-located to the United States and became known for intensity, friendliness, and enthusiasm

Answers: O, G, H, F, C, A, L, B, E, R, N, M, K, Q, I, J, P, D

7. **Twenty-Six Must Reads** (this semester, or whenever you make time!) Match the following published works with their authors.

A.	Maya Angelou	N.	B.F. Skinner
B.	Wallace Stevens	O.	Alexander Lowen
C.	Margery Williams Bianco	P.	Carl Jung
D.	Erik H. Erikson	Q.	Jean Baker-Miller
E.	Sigmund Freud	R.	Thomas Kuhn
F.	Carol Gilligan	S.	James MacGregor Burns
G.	William Glasser	T.	Thomas Moore
H.	Carl Rogers	U.	Irving Yalom
I.	Fritz Perls	V.	Alfred Adler
J.	Alice Miller	W.	Toni Morrison
K.	William James	X.	John B. Watson
L.	Aaron Beck	Y.	Carl Whitaker and Augustus Napier
M.	Rollo May	Z.	Rudolph Dreikurs

_P_ Symbols of Transformation (1956)
_X_ Behaviorism (1925)
_G_ Positive Addiction (1976)
_M_ The Courage to Create (1975)
_U_ Existential Psychotherapy (1981)
_E_ Civilization and Its Discontents (1930)
_I_ In and Out the Garbage Pail (1969)
_B_ The Palm at the End of the Mind (1972)
_W_ Beloved (1988)
_S_ Leadership (1978)
_V_ Social Interest: A Challenge to Mankind (1964, 1938)
_J_ Drama of the Gifted Child (1981)
_O_ The Betrayal of the Body (1967)
_K_ The Varieties of Religious Experience (1902)
_L_ Depression: Causes and Treatment (1972)
_D_ Identity and the Life Cycle (1980)
_N_ Beyond Freedom and Dignity (1971)

_C_ The Velveteen Rabbit (1922)
_R_ The Structure of Scientific Revolutions (1962)
_F_ In A Different Voice (1982)
_Q_ Toward a New Psychology of Women (1976)
_T_ Care of the Soul (1992)
_H_ On Becoming a Person (1961)
_A_ Wouldn't Take Nothing For My Journey Now (19..)
_Y_ The Family Crucible (1983)
_Z_ Children: The Challenge (1964)

Answers: P, X, G, M, U, E, I, B, W, S, V, J, O, K, L, D, N, C, R, F, Q, T, H, A, Y, Z

Part 3   Stages and Skills of Counseling   **133**

DANCING WITH THE INTERVENTIONS

CHAPTERS SEVEN, EIGHT, NINE & TEN

Hackney & Cormier

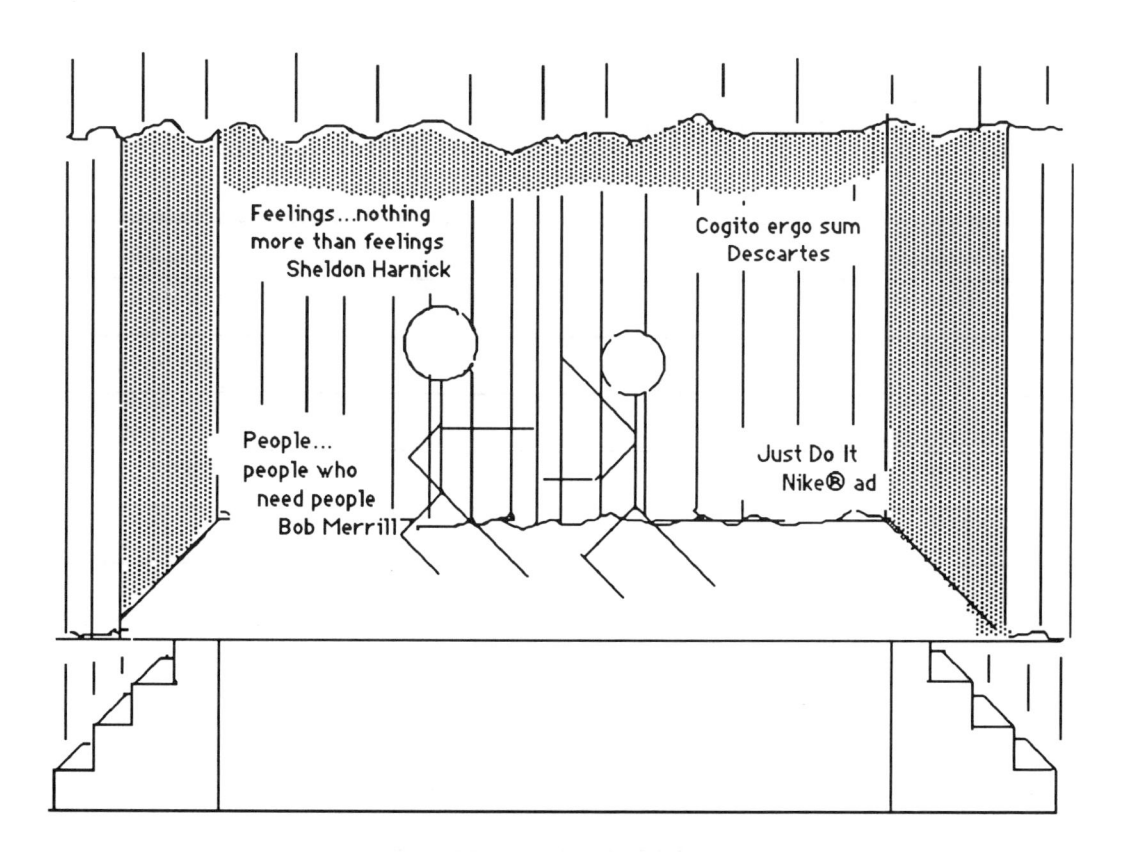

Feelings...nothing more than feelings
Sheldon Harnick

Cogito ergo sum
Descartes

People... people who need people
Bob Merrill

Just Do It
Nike® ad

. . . for analysis is always followed by synthesis,
and what was divided on a lower level
will reappear, united, on a higher one.
Carl Jung (Vol. 20, CW, ¶238)

134 Personal Workbook

Your textbook presents counseling as *process*. Consistent with that philosophy, we suggest that you think of your counselor education and training in the same way. A process of learning often includes first, an analysis (*-lysis*, a breaking up) followed by a synthesis (*-thesis*, a putting together). You might think of this evolution as deconstruction followed by reconstruction; dissolution followed by resolution.

1. **Re-read Chapters 7, 8, 9, and 10 in your textbook**. These chapters provide an analysis of *affective* interventions, *cognitive* interventions, *behavioral* interventions, and *systemic* interventions. After several readings of the chapters, use the following material to begin your synthesis of these four different approaches to counseling relative to *the person you are, your preferred ways of being in the world, and your worldview.*

   The human experience is far too complex to conceptualize solely via a view from one window. A person represents an orchestration of feelings, thoughts, behaviors, and systems of relationality. The effective counselor recognizes this and develops the ability to move fluidly among multiple views of clients and their lives. Again, we will all be naturally drawn to particular windows on the life experience and tend to be more comfortable paying attention to say, feelings first. But what would we miss if that was the only view we pursued?

   _____

   _____

   _____

   _____

   _____

   _____

   _____

   _____

   _____

   _____

   _____

   _____

   To add even more complexity, feelings and thoughts may not be clearly separated and distinct. Often the client's cognitions will bear a "feeling tone" and feelings may be intellectualized into thoughts. Furthermore, the culture of the individual will necessarily impact the ways in which particular windows of experience will be made available.

2. A useful way of beginning your synthesis might be to go back to the section of this workbook in which we looked at *content* versus *context* (p. 78).

      CONTENT - emphasizes the *concrete*

                emphasizes *product*

                emphasizes the *objective*

      CONTEXT - emphasizes the *abstract*

                emphasizes *process*

                emphasizes the *subjective*

Think of analysis as *content-focused*. As you read the textbook breakdown of the various interventions, consider the separate elements of each. What are the concrete goals of each?

_____

_____

_____

_____

_____

_____

_____

Next, think of synthesis as *context-focused*. How do the interventions relate to the uniqueness (i.e., the subjective natures) of both counselor and client? How would these interventions be experienced within the culture of the client?

_____

_____

_____

_____

_____

_____

_____

3. Edward T. Hall (1976; 1983) has discussed the nature of culture and has used the terms *content* and *context* to illustrate the ways individuals are enculturated to emphasize particular aspects of human experience.

Low Context (High Content) Cultures	High Context (Low Content) Cultures
Examples: Northern European, Scandinavian, Mainstream United States Caucasian	Examples: Mexican-American, African-American, some rural United States Caucasian
emphasis on material attainment (object)	emphasis on relational experience (subject)
more individual focus	more collective focus
time conceived of as linear (units)	time conceived of as circular (wholes)
microscopic view	macroscopic view
empirical fantasy	phenomenological fantasy
dichotomous logical reasoning	transcendent unifying reasoning

A. Obviously, no one is a product of any one culture. Due to colonization and the technologies of mobility and communication, persons are assimilated in varying degrees across cultures. For example, an individual may be Africocentric in terms of ethnic heritage and yet be more Caucasocentric in terms of operational identity. With this in mind, consider your own cultural heritage. How does your heritage relate to and/or differ from your core identity? Do you find yourself emphasizing low context values in one setting (e.g., work) and high context values in another setting (e.g., home life)? Or perhaps is the reverse true for you?

_____
_____
_____

B. How might these low context/high context cultural values impact the ways in which organize your counseling approach relative to the four interventions discussed in your textbook?

_____
_____
_____

C. Mark an "x" along the continuum where you see these interventions being more culturally identified:

Affective Interventions:

LOW CONTEXT _____ HIGH CONTEXT

Cognitive Interventions:

LOW CONTEXT _____ HIGH CONTEXT

Behavioral Interventions:

LOW CONTEXT _____ HIGH CONTEXT

Systemic Interventions:

LOW CONTEXT _____ HIGH CONTEXT

Part 3   Stages and Skills of Counseling **137**

D. Consider the case example of Angela in your textbook (p. 215). You encounter Angela as her counselor. Imagine the metaphor of meeting her on a dance floor. This would represent her field of experience.

   (1) How would you approach her?

   _____

   _____

   _____

   (2) What would cue you as to the indication of the most appropriate initial move?

   _____

   _____

   _____

   (3) How might your enculturation have influenced this clinical decision?

   _____

   _____

   _____

   (4) What would cue you as to the next move; and the next?

   _____

   _____

   _____

   (5) How would Angela's age, ethnic heritage, sexual orientation, and position of cultural assimilation impact the field of experience she presents? How might these same factors relative to you impact your approach to her?

   _____

   _____

   _____

   _____

138 Personal Workbook

4. **The Intervention Dance Floor**

   Here we present the analogy of dancing to encourage your process in the integration of interventions into your professional persona. In dancing there is a fluidity of movement. One leads, the other follows. Perhaps you will be a counselor to which feelings lead initially, but then cognitions will begin to lead as feelings follow. Suddenly the beat changes and behaviors take the lead. Well, you get the point.

   From the textbook, select a number of client profiles and imagine each as this client on the dance floor below. To which area of the floor would you be most naturally drawn in each scenario. Imagine yourself moving about the floor in step with the client's movements.

   Imagine yourself as counselor standing here ⬇   Let the music begin!

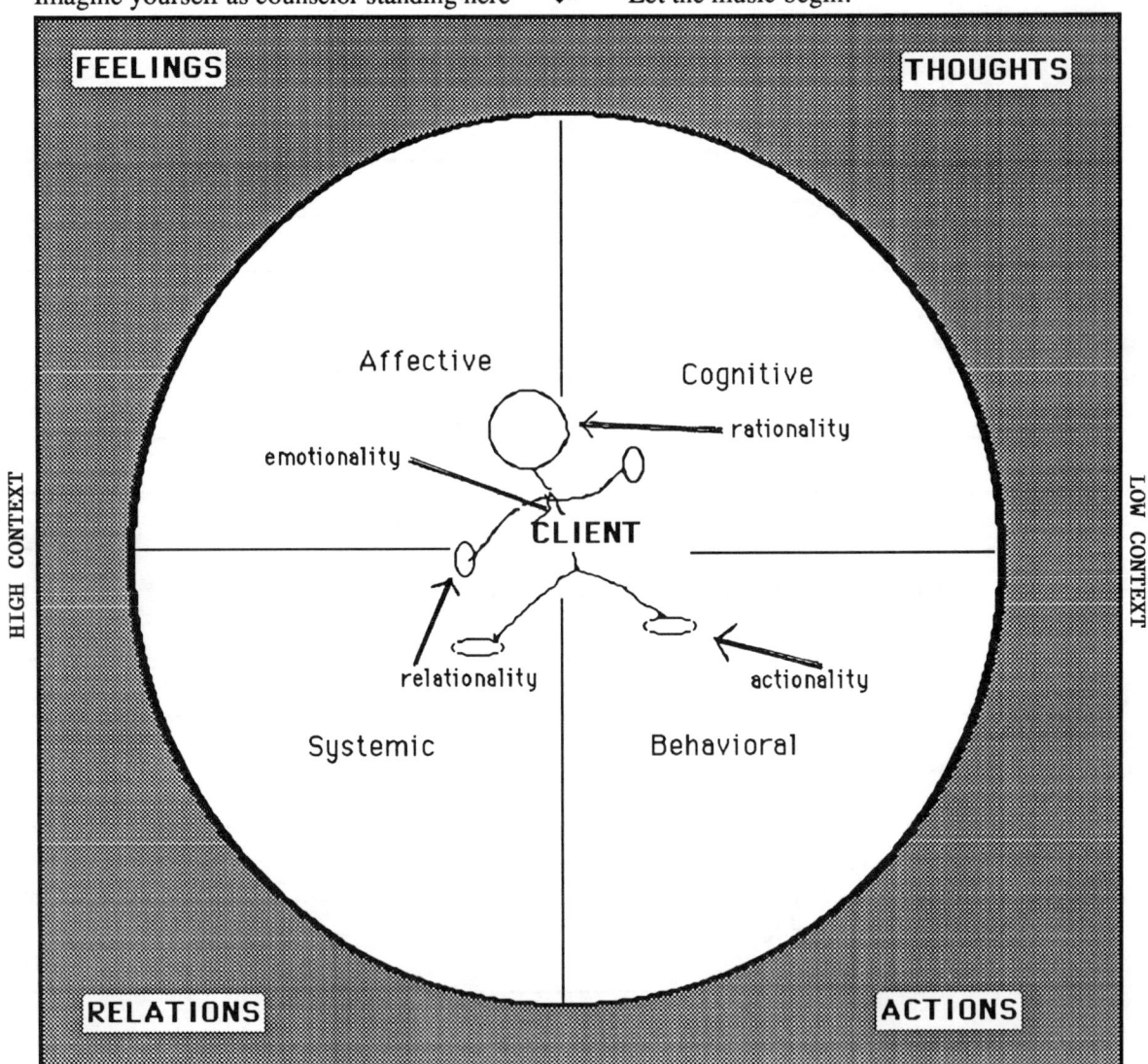

   FEELINGS — **THOUGHTS**

   Affective | Cognitive
   emotionality — rationality
   CLIENT
   relationality — actionality
   Systemic | Behavioral

   HIGH CONTEXT — LOW CONTEXT

   RELATIONS — **ACTIONS**

Part 3   Stages and Skills of Counseling **139**

A. Refer to the "Entering the Room" exercise on page 128. What connections do you see here with regard to your natural inclinations and the clinical interventions you would choose?

___

B. Refer to the "cultural assessment" you did beginning on page 25. What factors of your own history do you see that are influencing the intervention dance most comfortable for you?

___

C. How might these factors impact your intentional *leading* and *following* in the dance of intervention?

___

4. Re-consider the statement on page 191 of your textbook: "A general guideline for selecting counseling strategies is that clients are more receptive when the choice of strategy matches their experiencing of the problem."

A. Relative to the metaphor of dancing as strategy and intervention selection, what if the counselor's step is not consistent with the client's? In other words, what if the counselor is attempting to *waltz* and the client is doing a *two step*?

___

B. What perceptual faculties will you utilize to get in step with the client's experiencing of the problem(s) presented in counseling?

___

TERMINATION

CHAPTER ELEVEN

Hackney & Cormier

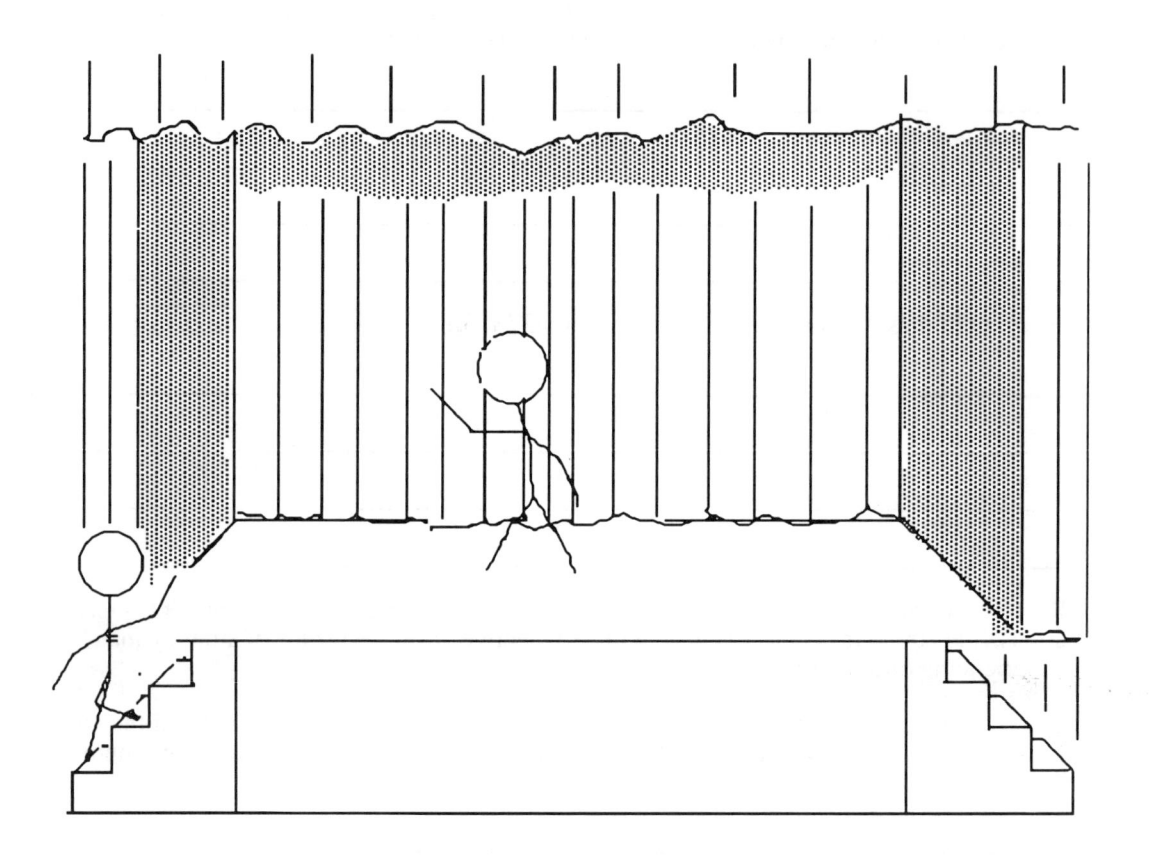

*We shall not cease from exploration
And the end of all our exploring
Will be to arrive where we started
And know the place for the first time.*
T.S. Eliot

1. **Breaking Up Is Hard To Do.**

A. Think back on particular relationships in which you have been involved that came to an end. List examples here:

_____

_____

_____

_____

B. What brought about the endings? How often was it due to extrinsic factors such as re-location, death, divorce? How often did you or the other person initiate the ending?

_____

_____

_____

_____

C. How did these endings serve as developmental transitions for you and the other person? In other words, what resources did you come to utilize as a result of the ending that you would not have known had the relationship continued?

_____

_____

_____

_____

D. How would you describe your particular styles of *attachment* and *separation*. See Bowlby (1969; 1973)

_____

_____

_____

_____

142   Personal Workbook

E.   Create a personal *loss line* for yourself. Between the time of your birth and the present day indicate along a line the significant losses you have experienced. Loss may be:

- *concrete* (e.g., loss of a person, money, house)

- *abstract* (e.g., loss of a dream, hope, possibility)

BIRTH   PRESENT

Imagine that you are standing in your present place and looking back down across time at these losses. How have you grieved each of them? What seems *finished; unfinished*? How might these experiences impact your willingness and ability to effectively terminate client relationships? For example, if you have lost a child to death in the past, how might termination with a client who is a child be different than terminating with an adult client?

_____

_____

_____

_____

Now, bend the loss line into a circle with you standing in the middle. Imagine that all of your losses are around you constantly with both their resolved and unresolved aspects

What seems different with time conceived of as circular rather than linear?

2. **Rituals of separation.** Transition points of birth and death have always been and will remain dramatic aspects of life *across cultures.* Frequently, individuals and groups have created rituals to mark these transitions. The *christening, Bris, Bar Mitzvah, graduation, wedding,* and *funeral* are all examples of culturally-expressed acknowledgments of beginnings and endings. What does a ritual intend to accomplish?

    - a meaningful emotional acknowledgment of some culturally significant event

    - a symbolic picture (metaphor) that one thing has ended and another has begun

    - a concretization of a complex constellation of feelings, thoughts, hopes, regrets, and ideals

    - often executed as a coming together of members of a culture for support, solace, celebration

   For example, the funeral intends to:

    - *confirm* the reality of a death

    - *celebrate* a life that has been lived

    - *collect* social support in a time of loss

    - *communicate* the values and beliefs of a culture relative to the event of death and beyond

   As a counselor you will invest much time and psychological capital in establishing *and* ending relationships. How you experience such transitions in general and especially how you experience them with clients will to a large degree determine the value of the experience to clients. How do you suppose so many beginnings and endings will impact you and your psychological health? In other words, how will you cope with on-going loss and *accrued* grief?

Just as people have done for centuries in dealing with dramatic transitions, counselors may also find it useful to employ ritual. Below is one example of how a counselor and client created a ritual to mark the termination of their relationship.

> The client, Mary, was a 28 year old woman who had come to counseling for assistance with grief issues surrounding the sudden death of her husband. The counselor, Helena, had been successful in nurturing strong rapport with Mary which led to a solid working alliance. Together they explored many aspects of the loss Mary had sustained. At one point Helena suggested that Mary begin writing letters to her deceased husband expressing a plethora of emotions and thoughts. Helena suggested that Mary keep the letters in a safe place until the counseling process could make its course. When time came for termination, Helena and Mary talked about the loss they were both feeling at their impending separation and Helena suggested that they develop a ritual to mark the transition. Mary was agreeable.
>
> Here's what they came up with. Mary brought all the letters to her next to last session. Helena made arrangements to have a paper shredder there. They opened the box and one by one shredded the letters   As they looked at the letters it was obvious how far Mary had come in her work with Helena and where she was now in terms of her grief recovery process. It was a tearful and at the same time joyous session.
>
> For the final session Helena and Mary decided that they would meet at a nearby park where they had made arrangements to plant a tree appropriate to the season and the region. All of the particulars were cleared with the park maintenance department who dug the hole, set the tree beside the hole, left two shovels, and ensured Helena and Mary of their privacy. Helena and Mary arrived at the appointed time and Mary brought the shredded letters from their previous session. Mary placed the shredded letters in the hole, soaked them with water from a hose provided by the park maintenance department, and together they lifted the tree down on top of the shredded paper that once held so much pain for Mary and now represented her release. Helena read passages from Thoreau's writings and Mary read a poem she had written.
>
> Alternating shovels of dirt, Helena and Mary said good-bye to each other.
> At the end of the hour, each entered their cars and went separate ways. They never saw each other again. The tree blossoms every springtime.

This ritual worked for Mary and Helena because it reflected their values as people and captured the emotional tone of death and re-birth for them.

There are some important caveats:

- Any ritual involving both client and counselor must be designed together.

- If the ritual is to be carried out outside the helping crucible, measures must be taken to ensure the safety and privacy of the client.

- Counselors must remind themselves that while the ritual is for both persons, it is the client's needs that remain paramount

- Thought must be given to details. For example in the ritual described above, Helena had instructed Mary to write the letters with water-soluble ink so as to not subject the roots of the tree to any toxic chemical such as lead from a pencil. Also, it is critical to make certain that a living thing such as a tree will be cared for.

There are ways for counselors to have "funerals" for client relationships in solitude; without the presence or even knowledge of the client. Here are some examples:

- Create a termination garden near your office and plant something each time you attach or separate with a client; perhaps *annuals* such as zinnias for attachment and *perennials* such as roses for termination. This symbolizes that attachment is temporary and separation is eternal. If you reside in an area with limited growing seasons, a rock garden is an idea. Colorful rocks to symbolize attachment and separation can provide striking imagery.

- Donate a book, anonymously, to a library or school each time you terminate with a client.

- Place a tree such as a *ficus* in your office. Each time you terminate with a client, pluck a leaf from the tree and place it in a bowl or urn to dry. At times throughout the year, take the container of dried leaves to a favorite stream or river. With meaningful poetry or prose, have a funeral. One by one, place the leaves into the running stream and watch them disappear into the distance.

- When you conclude a termination session with a client, open your window and release a balloon. Check local regulations first!

- Food is often a part of separation rituals. Each time you terminate with a client, take a bag of pet food to an animal shelter or donate canned goods to a food bank. Then, enjoy a meal for yourself and as you dine, reflect on the loss of the relationship just ended.

- What are some ideas for separation ritual come to you?

_____

_____

_____

_____

_____

_____

_____

_____

REMEMBER: TERMINATION IS A PROCESS, NOT AN EVENT. IT BEGINS AT INTAKE!

APPLYING COUNSELING SKILLS TO UNIQUE SITUATIONS
CHAPTER 12
Hackney & Cormier

*In order to represent life on the stage,
we must rub elbows with life, live ourselves.*
Marie Dressler

1. Think back on crisis situations you have personally experienced. List some examples here.

   _____

   _____

   _____

   _____

   _____

2. How do you respond to crisis? Some persons report that they are at their best under extreme circumstances. How is it for you?

   _____

   _____

   _____

   _____

   _____

3. Volunteer to work on a crisis call help-line operated by an agency in your area. Make certain that the agency provides a quality training experience for its volunteers.

4. Visit the Employee Assistance Program director for a corporation in your area. Discuss the goals of the program, its philosophy, and perceived impact on the organization.

5. Consider the value of balancing your counseling activities with professional efforts outside the traditional helping crucible. For example, think about how application of counseling principles could provide opportunities for you to do some teaching, advance the early intervention aspect of counseling, and allow a welcome departure from the intensity of one-to-one helping services.

6. Design a psycho-educational program on a topic of interest to you such as parenting, stress resolution, communication, relationship enhancement, or maybe, coping with graduate school. Ask your professor to allow you to present the program to your class.

7. Discuss with your professor and colleagues creative ways counseling can be made available to more persons.

PART FOUR

THE FOUNDATION OF IT ALL- A CODE OF ETHICS AND BEYOND

Appendix A

Hackney & Cormier

*We cast a shadow on something wherever we stand,
and it is no good moving from place to place to save things;
because the shadow always follows. Choose a place where you won't do harm
- yes, choose a place where you won't do very much harm,
and stand in it for all you are worth, facing the sunshine.*
E.M. Forster
A Room with a View

READ THE PREAMBLE AND SECTIONS OF THE
ACA CODE OF ETHICS AND STANDARDS OF PRACTICE,
***APPENDIX A* IN YOUR TEXTBOOK.**

1. What is ACA's definition of "Code of Ethics?"

   _____

   _____

   _____

2. What is ACA's definition of "Standards of Practice?"

   _____

   _____

   _____

3. What challenges might you face converting *principles* into *behaviors*?

   _____

   _____

   _____

   _____

   _____

4. A "code of ethics" is sometimes seen simply as a set of rules to be imposed on the members of a particular profession and enforced under the threat of punishment. Here, we take a different view. What follows below suggests that ethical behavior begins in the hearts and minds of the professional membership. It departs from moral preaching and suggests that healthy and happy professionals are much more unlikely to commit an ethical violation.

In our view the most effective counselor, and thus the most ethically operating, is:

- well nourished
- well rested
- secure in identity
- self esteeming
- physically healthy
- sexually satiated
- operating within optimal stressors
- living a life filled with loving relationships
- served by a vital sense of humor

As the young people of one era were fond of saying,

GET A LIFE!!!!!

Consider the differences of this approach to ethical behavior as compared to a rules and regulations approach.

COUNSELOR FITNESS MODEL	**RULES AND REGULATIONS MODEL**
ethical behavior derived from an internal function	ethical behavior derived from an external construct
prevailing control - needs met outside the professional relationship	prevailing control - the fear of punishment
ethical conduct a way of life	ethical conduct something to be enforced
ethical behavior a countertransference issue	ethical behavior an issue of defined good and evil

It appears that most often, when a breach of ethical conduct occurs in the counseling relationship, it is a case of the counselor's needs becoming involved and eventually taking precedence. This would suggest that the more *neediness* the counselor brings to the work the greater the chance of an ethical violation.

5. How do you re-create yourself? In behavioral terms, how do you play?

Counseling is a human activity and counselors are human beings. We make mistakes. It is our hope that you will take with you the probable correlation between the *wellness of the professional and the ethical practice of the profession.* At the end of each day, how will you re-create yourself? From what *re*-creational activities do you typically find the most *re*-freshment? What kinds of conditions will the stress of a day of counseling present that may require new means of re-creation? For example, you may now find that walking and talking with a good friend about the day and its activities is helpful. Now, you are entering a profession where you will be unable to talk with anyone about your work. How will you handle this?

_____

_____

_____

_____

_____

_____

_____

_____

_____

_____

From the above examples of ways you re-create yourself, how might they be adapted to your new life as a professional counselor?

_____

_____

_____

_____

_____

_____

_____

6. Highly recommended reading is a book by Grosch & Olsen (1994) entitled *When Helping Starts To Hurt*. Below is an excerpt:

> Most of us entered the helping professions with high ideals and generous hearts. Armed with our own particular brand of salvation, we were going to change the world, or at least some of the people in it. We didn't become therapists or counselors to make money, but to help people. We started out with enormous optimism and what we thought was sufficient training and expertise. We firmly believed that this training, along with compassion and caring, would enable us to transform the lives of people who were hurting. Sadly, for many of us, idealism, optimism, and commitment gave way to disillusion and disappointment. The reality that, contrary to expectation, many of our well-intentioned efforts were ineffective and unappreciated came as a bitter irony and left us terribly disappointed. Now many of us who started out hoping to make a difference in the world have ended up hoping simply to make it to the end of the day. (p. ix)

Recalling the maxim derived from the work of Maslow that "under stress we regress," consider how a tired, needy, frustrated, and deluded counselor is more likely to violate an ethical boundary and become involved with a client in a dual relationship, a sexual relationship, discuss clients carelessly outside the helping crucible, or in any other manner bring harm to the personhood of the client.

A. Think about the areas of your life that are currently presenting the most stress.

_____
_____
_____
_____
_____
_____

B. How might these aspects translate into chances for ethical violations with your clients? In other words, where are you the most vulnerable?

_____
_____
_____
_____
_____
_____

Remember the old Liberian proverb:

Do not look where you fell, but where you slipped.

Part 4 The Foundation of It All - A Code of Ethics and Beyond

7. Consider the ways a "code of ethics" intends to protect: Refer to Mabe & Rollin (1986).

A. the profession _____

_____

_____

_____

_____

the counselor _____

_____

_____

_____

_____

the consumer _____

_____

_____

_____

_____

B. If a profession states that it is able to govern itself without outside (e.g., governmental) regulation, some argue that this is a case of "the mice guarding the cheese." What do you think about this?

_____

_____

_____

_____

D. How might a profession encourage its members to establish and maintain a constant state of responsibility *TO* its clients without suggesting that it is responsible *FOR* them?

_____

_____

_____

_____

8. Counselors are faced with ethical dilemmas each and every day. Rarely are the resolutions clean and simple. For example, you may find yourself caught between the law and your own values; or between institutional policy and your worldview. It is useful to have a structure around which to assemble your concerns. Van Hoose (1980, pp. 10-11) has provided such a schema. (See also Herlihy & Golden, 1990)

- *What is the problem or dilemma?*

    This is the one that often gives counselors the most difficulty. Perhaps because counselors either by temperament or training or both are given to thinking in possibilities, reducing a complex ethical dilemma down to a defined problem that is manageable is quite a task.

- *Do any guiding principles exist to help resolve the dilemma?*

    Here the Code of Ethics and Standards of Practice are consulted. Remember, these are not "rules" as such, but are guidelines to be considered within the context of the ethical dilemma. If the dilemma presents a conflict between say the law and ethics, it may be necessary to consult in confidence with experts on both sides (i.e., an attorney to illuminate the legal side and a trusted colleague in counseling relative to the ethics involved. We all have blind spots and the gift of trusted colleagues for consultation in such matters as ethical concerns in invaluable.

- *What are the possible and probable courses of action?*

    Given the extant conditions of the ethical dilemma you are attempting to resolve, what can be done?

- *What are the potential consequences for each course of action?*

    Certainly all actions have consequences. What actions provide the greatest amount of resolve and the least amount of damage to all parties involved?

- *What is the best course of action?*

    Again, counselors are notorious for processing *ad infinitum* . At some point, it is necessary to take action!

Now, assemble a small group of your colleagues and consider the following ethical dilemmas. Using the Van Hoose schema and *Appendix A* of the textbook, work through to some resolution. Assume that all of the counselors involved are members of ACA and thus bound by its Code of Ethics and Standards of Practice.

AN UNEASY VICTORY

Mary S., a woman in her late thirties presented herself for counseling reporting an unhappy marriage, low self-esteem, feelings of depression, and fear of establishing trusting relationships with others. The counselor, an RET therapist, challenged Mary's irrational beliefs about herself and her negative self-talk. She encouraged Mary to begin circulating more and to take an assertiveness training course. Mary did both. One day when Mary came in for her session she seemed renewed, refreshed, and invigorated. When the therapist inquired as to the nature of her "new face" Mary replied, "Well, I know I can trust you and there was a time when I didn't feel I could, but well, I've met a wonderful man and we are falling in love. I feel like a teen-ager and I have you to thank."

As the session progressed Mary disclosed the identity of the man with whom she had become involved. He was the husband of one the counselor's closest friends.

THE COMPROMISED COUNSELOR

Martin C., a respected counselor for more than fifteen years was observed by his colleagues to be consistently tired and irritable. To any inquiry from his concerned associates he replied curtly that his caseload had grown considerably and that he was putting in some long hours. Then it became obvious that he was coming to work intoxicated and was often late for sessions. Two colleagues who shared office space and trusting relationships with Martin confronted him and insisted that he get some help. Martin exploded, ordered them out of his office, and told them to mind their own business.

THE COUNSELOR'S NEW TOY

Cindy, a skilled counselor, attended a week-long workshop presenting a particular type of therapy about which she had been reading. She experienced the presentation as "phenomenal." Upon returning home to her practice, she could not wait to see her clients and begin trying out the techniques and skills she had acquired at the workshop.

___

THE ENTREPRENEURIAL COUNSELOR

David, a well-established counselor, decided that he wanted to expand his professional activity and increase his income by doing workshops and seminars in the community. He was known for his work with anxiety disorders and thus this was the area on which he intended to focus. Sensitive about advertising he concluded that he could fill considerable space with his clients. He printed up flyers and handed them out during sessions. When clients seemed less than enthusiastic about the activity, David lectured them about only being able to be helped if they took advantage of every available resource, and maybe after all, "They just didn't want help."

Part 4   The Foundation of It All - A Code of Ethics and Beyond **155**

THE INDIGESTED COUNSELOR

Pat, a busy counselor, scheduled a luncheon with an associate she had not seen for a while. At 11:00, they met at a restaurant known for its rich food and generous portions. The two shared appetizers and Pat, who had been working very hard, ordered a large entree along with heavenly chocolate cheesecake for dessert. The food was savory and it was good to catch up with an old friend. Regretfully, Pat had to cut the get-together short because of a 1:00 appointment with a client.

THE CLEAN BUT CARELESS COUNSELOR

Richard, a counselor in private practice, decided that he needed some help to keep the office clean. He engaged the assistance of a professional cleaning service. Subject to the agreement, the cleaning people would come in at night and do the office. Richard, tired at the end of a busy day and thinking how good it was to have someone to tidy up, left several folders of client records on his desk.

THE PROUD BUT INSENSITIVE GRANDPARENT

Edith, a successful counselor for over thirty years had recently become a grandmother. She virtually filled her office with photos of the new baby. Edith specialized in grief counseling, and she thought the pictures of this beautiful child were life-affirming additions to her counseling setting. At the time Edith was seeing several clients who had lost young children to death.

ASSAULT ON PRIVACY

Carlos, a well-known counselor, was browsing through the super-market one day and he spotted one of his clients who appeared to be shopping alone. A friendly, out-going man, Carlos rushed up behind the client and said jokingly, "I'm following you!" The startled client turned around and saw Carlos. Her response seemed awkward and grew even more so as she tried to introduce Carlos to the man who had now appeared and was obviously her shopping companion. The man was her husband and he did not know she was in counseling.

Thus, this workbook ends just as it began: with the emphasis on you and your overall fitness for the grueling work of counseling.

Part 4   The Foundation of It All - A Code of Ethics and Beyond **157**

Now, whether you are traveling, making an odyssey,
Or some contextually-defined combination of the two,
Go on your way rejoicing,
open to the challenges that a rigorous counselor education will present you -
And take these words of Shakespeare with you:

> Sweet are the uses of adversity,
> Which, like the toad, ugly and venomous,
> Wears yet a precious jewel in his head.
> And this our life, exempt from public haunt,
> Finds tongues in trees, books in running brooks,
> Sermons in stones, and good in every thing.
>
> *As You Like It*
> *Act 2, Scene 1; Line 12*

References

Adler, A. (1938). *Social interest: A challenge to mankind.* London: Faber and Faber.

Adler, A. (1958).*What life should mean to you.* New York: Capricorn Books.

Alschuler, C. F., & Alschuler, A. S. (1984). Developing health responses to anger: The counselor's role. *Journal of Counseling and Development, 63,* 26-29.

Angelou, M. (1993). *Wouldn't take nothing for my journey now.* New York: Random House.

Aubrey, R. (1983). The Odyssey of counseling and images of the future. *Personnel and Guidance Journal, 62,* 78-82.

Baker, H. S. (1987). Heinz Kohut's self pscyhology: An overview. *American Journal of Psychiatry, 144,* 5.

Beck, A. T. (1972). *Depression: Causes and treatments.* Philadelphia: University of Pennsylvania Press.

Bianco, M. W. (1922). *The velveteen rabbit; of, How toys become real.* London: Heinemann.

Bordin, E. S. (1983). A working alliance based model of supervision. *The Counseling Psychologist, 11,* 35-42.

Brickman, P., Rabinowitz, V. C., Karuza, J., Jr. Coates, D., Cohn, E., & Kidder, L., (1982). Models of helping and coping. *American Psychologist, 37,* 368-384.

Brown, D., Pryzwansky, W. B., & Schulte, A. C. (1994). *Psychological consultation: iIntroduction to theory and practice* (3rd ed.). Boston: Allyn & Bacon.

Burns, J. M. (1978). *Leadership.* New York: Harper & Row.

Consulting Psychologists Press. (1995). Myers-Briggs Type Indicator. Palo Alto: Consulting Psychologists Press.

Corcoran, K. J. (1981). Experiential empathy: A theory of a felt-level exerience. *Journal of Humanistic Psychology, 21,* 29-37.

Corey, G., Corey, M. S., & Callanan, P. (1993). *Issues and ethics in the helping professions..* Pacific Grove, CA: Brooks Cole Publishing Co.

D'Andrea, M. (1984). The counselor as pacer: A model for revitalization of the counseling profession. *Counseling and Human Development, 17,* 385-395.

Dreikurs, R. (1964). *Children: The challenge.* New York: Hawthorn/Dutton.

Eliot, G. (1860). *Adam Bede.* New York: Harper.

Erikson, E. H. (1980). *Identity and the life cycle.* New York: W. W. Norton.

Festinger, L. A. (1957). *A theory of cognitive dissonance.* Evanston,IL: Row, Perterson.

Freud, S. (1986). New introductory lectures on psycho-analysis. In J. Strachey (Ed. and Trans.), *The standard edition of the complete psychological works of Sigmund Freud* (Vol. 22). London, England: Hogarth Press. (Original work published 1933)

Freud, S. (1961). Civilization and its discontents (Strachey, J., Trans.). New York: W. W. Norton.

Gendlin, E. T. (1962). Experiencing and the creation of meaning. New York: Free Press of Glencoe.

Gilligan, C. (1982). *In a different voice: Psychological theory and women's development.* Cambridge, Mass.: Harvard University Press.

Glasser, W. (1976). *Positive addiction.* New York: Harper & Row.

Gordon, D. (1988). The role of language in therapy. In J. K. Zeig, (Ed.), *Developing Ericksonian therapy: State of the art.* (pp. 164-165). New York: Brunner/Mazel.

Grosch, W. N. & Olsen, D. C. (1994). *When helping starts to hurt: A new look at burnout among psychotherapists.* New York: W. W. Norton.

Gummere, R. M. (1988). The counselor as prophet: Frank Parsons, 1854-1908. *Journal of Counseling and Development, 66,* 402-405.

Hall, E. T. (1976). *Beyond culture.* Garden City, NY: Anchor Press.

Hall, E. T. (1983). *The dance of life: The other dimension of time.* Garden City, NY: Anchor Press/Doubleday.

Harris, M. (1986). Homer's Odyssey: A psychological journey. *American Journal of Psychoanalysis, 46,* 289-299.

Hillman, J. (1975). *Re-visioning psychology.* New York: Harper & Row.

James, W. (1902). *The varieties of religious experience.* New York: Modern Library.

Jewell, T. L., (1993). *The Black woman's gumbo ya-ya: Quotations by black women..* Freedom, CA: The Crossing Press.

Jung, C. G. (1956). *Symbols of transformation: An analysis of the prelude to a case of schizophrenia.* London: Routledge & K. Paul.

Jung, C. G. (1980). *Psychological types. CW6.* Princeton, NJ: Princeton University Press (Original work published 1923)

Kerényi, K. (1987). Hermes guide of souls: The mythologem of the masculine source of life (Stein, M., Trans.). Dallas: Spring Publications.

Kohut, H., (1971). The analysis of the self: A systematic approach to the psychoanaylitic treatment of narcissistic personality disorders. (*The Psychoanalytic study of the child, Monograph,. 4*). New York: International Universities Press.

Kohut, H., (1977). *The restoration of the self.* New York: International Universities Press.

Kuhn, T. S. (1962). *The structure of scientific revolutions.* Chicago: University of Chicago Press.

Loevinger, J. (1976). *Ego development.* San Francisco: Jossey-Bass.

Lowen, A. (1967). *The betrayal of the body.* New York: Macmillan.

Mabe, A. R. & Rollin, S. A. (1986). The role of a code of ethical standards in counseling. *Journal of Counseling and Development, 64,* 294-297.

Margolis, R. L. & Rungta, S. A. (1986). Training counselors for work with special populations: A second look. J*ournal of Counseling and Development, 64,* 642-644.

Marx, M. H., & Cronan-Hillix, W. A. (1987). *Systems and theories in psychology* (4th. ed.). New York: McGraw-Hill.

May, R. (1975). *The courage to create.* New York: W. W. Norton.

McGoldrick, M., & Gerson, R. (1985). *Genograms in family assessment.* (1st. ed.) New York: Norton.

Miller, A. (1981). *The drama of the gifted child* (Ward, R., Trans.). New York: Basic Books.

Miller, J. B. (1976). *Toward a new psychology of women.* Boston: Beacon Press.

Moore, T. (1992). *Care of the soul: A guide for cultivating depth and sacredness in everyday life.* New York: HarperCollins.

Morrison, T. (1987). *Beloved.* New York: Knopf.

Myers, L. J., Speight, S. L., Highlen, P. S., Cox, C. I., Reynolds, A. L. Adams, E. M., & Hanley, C. P., (1991). Identity development and worldview: Toward an otimal conceptualization. *Journal of Counseling and Development, 70,* 54-63.

Napier, A. & Whitaker, C. A. (1978). *The family crucible.* New York: Harper & Row.

Oxford English Dictionary (2d ed.). (1989). Oxford: Clarendon Press.

Perls, F. S. (1969). *In and out the garbage pail.* Moab, Utah: Real People Press.

Peterson, D. R. (1976). Is psychology a profession? *American psychologist, 31,* 572-581.

Pistole, M. C. (1989). Attachment: Implications for counselors. *Journal of Counseling and Development, 68,* 109-193.

Random House Dictionary of the English Language, (2nd ed., unabridged). (1987). New York: Random House.

Remley, T. P. (1992). Are counselors unique? *Guidepost, 35(2),* 4.

Rilke, R. M. (1984). *Letters to a young poet*t. New York: Random House.

Rogers, C. R. (1957). The necessary and sufficient conditions of theraeutic personality change. *Journal of Consulting Psychology, 21,* 95-103.

Rogers, C. R. (1961). *On becoming a person: A therapist's view of psychotherapy. Boston:* Houghton Mifflin.

Romanovsky, R. & Philips, P. (1989). Love is all it takes. *Be Political, Not Polite.*

Sargent, A. (Screenwriter), Schwary, L. (Producer), & Redford, R. (Director). (1980). *Ordinary people.* [Film].

Skinner, B. F. (1971). *Beyond freedom and dignity.* New York: Knopf.

Shipley, J. T. (1945). *Dictionary of word origins*. New York: The Philosophical Library.

Statistical Abstract of the United States. (1995). Washington, D. C.: U.S. Government Printing Office.

Stevens, Wallace. (1972). *The palm at the end of the mind* (Stevens, H., Ed.). New York: Vintage Books.

Strupp, H. H. (1974). On the basic ingredients of psychotherapy. *Psychotherapy & Psychosomatics, 24*, 249-260.

Sullivan, H. S. (1954). *The psychiatric interview*. New York: W. W. Norton.

Van Hoose, W. H. (1980). Ethics and counseling. *Counseling and Human Development, 13,* 1-12.

New York: W. W. Norton.

encapsulated counselor. *Harvard Educational Review, 32*, 444-449.

chotherapy. New York: Basic Books.